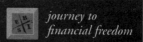

Rich Dad®   *journey to financial freedom*

My poor dad often said, "What you know is important." My rich dad said, "If you want to be rich, <u>who</u> you know is more important than <u>what</u> you know."

Rich Dad explained further saying, "Business and investing are team sports." The average investor or small-business person loses financially because they do not have a team. Instead of a team, they act as individuals who are trampled by very smart teams.

That is why the Rich Dad's Advisors book series was created. Rich Dad's Advisors will offer guidance to help you know who to look for and what kind of questions to ask so you can gather your own great team of advisors.

The ABC's of Real Estate Investing

The secrets of finding hidden profits most investors miss

Ken McElroy

WARNER
BUSINESS
BOOKS™

NEW YORK   BOSTON

Published by Warner Books in association with CASHFLOW® Technologies, Inc., and BI Capital Inc.

CASHFLOW, Rich Dad, Rich Dad's Advisors, Rich Dad's Seminars, the BI Triangle, and CASHFLOW Quadrant (ESBI Symbol) are registered trademarks of CASHFLOW® Technologies, Inc. Rich Kid Smart Kid, Rich Dad Australia, Rich Dad's Coaching, and Journey to Financial Freedom are trademarks of CASHFLOW® Technologies, Inc.

   are registered trademarks of CASHFLOW® Technologies, Inc.

Visit our Web site at www.richdad.com

Warner Business Books

Time Warner Book Group, 1271 Avenue of the Americas, New York, NY 10020.
Visit our Web site at: www.twbookmark.com.

The Warner Business Books logo is a trademark of Warner Books.

Printed in the United States of America

First Printing: September 2004
10   9   8   7   6   5   4

Library of Congress Cataloging-in-Publication Data

McElroy, Ken.
   The ABC's of real estate investing : the secrets of finding hidden profits most investors miss / Ken McElroy.—1st Warner Books printing
         p.   cm.—(Rich dad's advisors series)
      ISBN 0-446-69184-4
      1. Real estate investment—Handbooks, manuals, etc.   I. Title.   II. Series.
   HD1382.5.M295   2004
   332.63'24—dc22   2004008290

Acknowledgments

This book is dedicated to my wonderful wife, Laura, and my high-spirited boys, Kyle and Kade. Thank you all for your constant support and understanding as this book was being written.

I would like to thank Kathy Heasley, who was instrumental in extracting fifteen years of my investment real estate and property management knowledge and wonderfully organizing it into each chapter of this book (www.imsbreakthrough.com.).

Special thanks are also extended to Robert and Kim Kiyosaki and to Sharon Lechter for allowing me to participate as a Rich Dad's Advisor, and of course to my partner, Ross McCallister, for never saying anything other than encouraging words as I took on this venture.

Contents

Learn from an Expert

Go to any bookstore, and you will find there are many books written on the subject of investing in real estate. If you are like me, you may have read several of them. While the books are written by people who claim to be financially successful, I notice that many of them are not really real estate professionals.

One famous real estate author made a lot of money selling his real estate investment books, yet, in reality, he lost most of his money in real estate. Today, he continues to earn a lot of money selling his books and charging a lot of money for his seminars. Another famous author was a garage mechanic only a few years ago. He got into real estate after being fired from his job. Another book is written by an ex-banker who now sells his secrets on how to find foreclosure properties from banks. I recently ran into an ex-financial planner who stopped selling mutual funds after the stock market crash and is now holding seminars, teaching his investment secrets, and then getting his audience to invest in his high-priced properties.

The Rich Dad Company asked Ken McElroy to write this book for five reasons:

1. Ken is a real estate professional. Right out of college, he began his career as a property manager. Today, Ken McElroy owns one of the largest property management companies in the southwestern United States. Ken is also a developer of multimillion-dollar commercial properties, the president of the Arizona Multihousing Association, and is active in lobbying Congress for the real estate industry. Due to his track record and reputation, investment bankers such as Lehman Brothers are often Ken's financial partners in his projects.

2. Property management is one the most important aspects of real estate investing. Many people do not get into real estate investing—even though in my opinion it is the best investment class in the world—because they do not want to fix toilets or deal with tenants. I do not blame them. Ken's insight into the management side of real estate investing is priceless.

3. Property management is a long-term process. Finding a property, financing a property, and selling a property are, in most cases, relatively short-term events. If you are a true investor, rather than a speculator who flips properties for profits, the management of property is an ongoing process. In other words, the core of real estate is a long-term process of property management.

4. Property management is where most of the profits are made or lost. Many people lose money in real estate simply because they fail to manage their properties properly. If they cannot control the occupants, income, and expenses, the property soon goes downhill. The good news is that professional real

estate investors love buying properties from investors who fail to manage their properties well. Why? Because you can often buy the property at a good price and then, with good management skills, you can increase the cash flow as well as the value of the property.

5. Ken McElroy is a great teacher. Ken McElroy is not only a Rich Dad Advisor—for he does advise me on my property investments—we are also partners in several property investments. Most important to you, he is a great teacher who knows what he is talking about. Ken often accompanies me to speak to large groups, where he talks about how to manage property, how to analyze an investment, and how to tell whether or not the seller or broker is telling you the truth. If you ever have an opportunity to hear Ken speak about investing in real estate, take it.

As I said, there are many books on real estate investing and many people claiming to be real estate experts. What makes this book different is, first, it is written from the most important aspect of real estate investment, which is property management; and second, this book is written by a *real* expert.

—Robert Kiyosaki

The ABC's
of Real Estate Investing

The Myths and the Magic

In every business and every industry there are people who just seem to drip with success. They seem to know all the right people, make all the right decisions, be in all the right places at exactly the right time. They seem destined for success whether they even try or not. Real estate investing is no different. In every city or town, there seem to be real estate tycoons that struck it rich through real estate.

These are the people who just make success look easy. They appear confident, knowledgeable, savvy, and seem to see opportunities where others don't. It's easy for onlookers to think the achievements of these golden few are the result of luck or some sort of magic. But magic and luck have absolutely nothing to do with it.

About fifteen years ago, I decided I was going to be one of the people I just described. I was going to make my own success, be my own boss, and achieve financial freedom. And I chose property management as my route. Call it instinct, call it impatience, call it burning desire. I wasn't about to wait for a lucky break or a magic charm. I set out to make my dream happen, and I did it through action.

In the early days of my first property management and real estate deals, there was a lot of trial and error and I made my share of mistakes. But for every one mistake I made, I learned ten lessons and got smarter every day. I started to see patterns, discover formulas and systems, and develop a network of people I could count on. It took time and it took work, but the more I pursued my dream, the luckier I felt and the more often magical opportunities presented themselves to me.

Maybe there is a bit of luck and magic in success. But it's luck and magic that comes from working hard and being prepared. At the Rich Dad Seminars, where I often speak, I see people all the time who are taking the first steps toward future success, much like I did nearly two decades ago. Many have what it takes: the drive and desire that will help them overcome obstacles and be prepared.

Unfortunately, I also see at the seminars some who lack what it takes. They are the ones looking to get rich quick and have little or no idea of the commitment required to achieve business success. Others have a lot of desire, but lack the technical skill and the knowledge that can only come from experience. I wrote this book for them. This is not a get-rich-quick book. It is not a book written to motivate, although I hope you'll be inspired to follow your real estate investment dreams. Instead, it is a book that will disclose proven methods, remove the unknowns, and shorten the learning curve for anyone who chooses investment real estate as his or her path to financial freedom.

Before we get too deep into the how to's of finding, buying, and managing investment property, let's take some time to drive out a few myths, myths that if you buy into them, will only hold you back. I think you'll find the following list familiar. Have you or others said these very things? Are any of these statements echoing in your head and preventing you from moving forward? Are these untruths paralyzing you with fear? Let's get rid of them right up front. It's time to dump the baggage!

Myth #1: You Have to Already Be Wealthy to Invest in Real Estate

People think they need to have a large lump sum of money to invest in real estate. They think it is like saving for their first home or that it's something they can only do once they have made their fortune elsewhere. Both of these thoughts couldn't be further from the truth. You don't need hundreds of thousands of dollars in the bank to invest in real estate and you certainly don't need millions. All you need is a good real estate deal that makes sense—one that has profit potential and is based on solid financials.

My partner and I have been working this way for years. My very first investment deal was a condo that I bought furnished and rented out. It was a two-bedroom unit that I put into a rental program. People who wanted to get away from it all could call up and rent my condo or one of a hundred others for a weekend getaway. A cool $116,000 was what I paid and I put down $20,000 out of my own pocket. You're probably thinking, "See, I knew you had to have some cash to get started in this business."

Well, I did that deal before I knew better. Contrast that with a more recent acquisition of a 182-unit apartment complex in Sun City, Arizona. The total cost was $9 million. Before you close the book and say, this is out of my league, let me finish the story. The down payment was $2 million, which we raised from other investors. My out-of-pocket was zip. I gave the majority of the ownership to the people who lent me the down payment; in essence, I formed a partnership with them. My salesmanship had nothing to do with it. The deal was the hero; it was so good that people wanted to be a part of it. What I've come to know is that there are a lot of people looking for good real estate deals.

Some people are partner-averse, but I think partners are valuable. They help you spread your risk by allowing you to own smaller positions in a number of properties rather than a big position in just one. And it's a fact that teams accomplish more. As for the return? Which deal would you rather do, the $116,000 property that cost you $20,000? Or the one that cost you nothing and yielded you 10 percent of a $9 million deal? For the record, that's $900,000 and I'd choose the latter any day of the week.

Once you have located a real estate opportunity, the task is finding investors who are looking to earn a good return on their money. The first deal you do, granted, is the most difficult, because you are an unproven entity. But trust me: It gets easier and easier with every successful deal you put together.

All things are difficult before
they are easy.

Today, my partner and I have people literally standing in line who want to invest in our next real estate venture. Not because we're anything special. But because we are thorough. We look at a lot of deals and choose only the ones that are financially viable like the one above. We also communicate with our investors and treat them fairly. They make money when we make money.

You may be surprised to learn that there are plenty of people interested in investing in real estate, particularly when other investment vehicles like the stock market and bonds are flat or declining. Just look around at a Rich Dad Seminar. There are thousands of people in every city in which we speak who are looking for real estate investment deals that make sense. One of the people in a Rich Dad Seminar could be your first investment partner.

Myth #2: You Need to Start Small—Big Deals Are Too Risky

There is nothing wrong with starting small. Perhaps you're thinking about buying a $250,000 single-family home and making it a rental property. Or even a $320,000 duplex. But why rule out a $2 million, fifty-unit building? Believe it or not, any of these properties are within your reach.

Of course right now you're thinking, "No way! I can't afford a $2 million mortgage!" And to that I say, you may be right, but you don't have to be able to afford it. Here's why. Mortgages on smaller properties like single-family homes are almost always guaranteed through the buyer's own personal earning potential and wealth. You may be surprised to learn that larger investment property loans are secured by the asset itself. In other words, instead of the $2 million building riding on your own wealth, it is riding on its own valuation. This already is less risk to you.

Let's look at the previous example. The condo I purchased for $116,000 with a $20,000 out-of-pocket down payment was 100 percent my responsibility from mortgage to management. The $9 million project that I owned 10 percent of for no out-of-pocket cost was actually less risky because I had no cash invested and the property was professionally managed. The other property was mine, all mine—for better and for worse. Five years later, I sold the condo for $121,000, a gain of $5,000. Recently we refinanced the 182-unit building, which we had owned less than a year. Its newly appraised value was $11.3 million, more than $2 million above what we paid for it. And since I own 10 percent of the project, I made over $200,000 in less than a year. A testament to the power of buying and managing right and managing well.

This example also demonstrates risk related to valuation. When you buy a house or condo and rent it out, appreciation of the property rests solely on the appreciation of the surrounding neighborhood. You better have bought in the right neighborhood, because there is little you can do to increase the value of your property. By contrast, appreciation in commercial property, like apartment buildings, is based on the cash flow of the property itself. The more money it makes, the more money it is worth. Now you're in control! When cash flow increases so does the value of the property. Manage your property right and you'll increase the value. Don't manage it right, and the value will stay the same or go down.

Another way larger properties are less risky relates to occupancy. When a single-family home is rented, it's 100 percent occupied. When it is empty, it is 100 percent vacant, and you are covering the mortgage out of your own pocket in its entirety. In a larger property, even an eight-unit building, if one resident leaves, you still have seven residents paying rent. Your exposure related to occupancy is greatly reduced the more residents you have.

Myth #3: You Can "Flip" Your Way to Success or Get Rich Quick with No Money Down

Many people think that flipping property, in other words buying it and quickly turning around and selling it for more than you paid for it, is the way to grow wealth. The people who believe strongly in this have been lucky enough to make money this way. But in my opinion, this is like day trading in the stock market. It isn't easy, and it is very risky.

No money down is another way of saying that the property is 100 percent financed. That means a much larger part, if not all, of your cash flow is going toward the monthly payment. In no-money-down deals, you'll be paying higher interest rates because there is greater risk to the lender, have higher loan costs, and have virtually no money to improve the property or even repair it should something break. With this model, you are banking on the property appreciating to make money rather than improving the operations of the property and making money through cash flow. Let's hope the market is high-flying and that you time it perfectly because you'll be banking on external factors being just right. Appreciation, as you'll see in great detail later, is only in your control when you've improved cash flow. In this scenario you have none!

As you might have guessed, I don't believe in zero dollars down, and I don't believe in flipping property. Even in the example where I personally put no cash down on the $9 million apartment building in Sun City, we as an investment team put $2 million down. I believe that buying and holding income-generating assets like rental properties is how you build wealth. You may say, "But I need the capital gain—the additional equity I've made on this property—to buy a second bigger rental property with more units. That means I have to sell the first one." In my experience this just isn't true. What you need is a second investment deal that makes sense that you can bring to investors. They will help you raise the down payment on the second property and you will reward them as the investment makes money.

We recently finished construction of a 208-unit property located in Goodyear, Arizona, which cost us $13.8 million to build. Upon completion it appraised for $16.3 million. We have received numerous offers to sell this property and brokers were standing in line for the listing. As tempting as it was to walk away after two years' work with $2.5 million in cash, we did not sell it. The problem is one of taxation. Had we taken the $2.5 million gain, we would have been forced to place that money back in the market to avoid a pretty hefty tax bill. Sure we had appreciation, but we also had what is known as a "taxable event." Imagine the tax bill of 30 percent on a $2.5 million gain. That's an unnecessary $750,000 tax payment.

If you want the money out, you don't need to sell. You refinance the property and pull out what equity you can. There is no taxable event, and you are not forced to put the money into another investment. In the case of the 208-unit property, we will refinance and we will use the equity that we pulled out of the property to pay back our investors with interest. It's a great system and best of all you still own the property, you continue to receive cash flow from the building in the form of rent, and as the building appreciates, you can refinance and take the gain—tax-free—again. That's the money that you can use for other deals and it's what I do every day.

Property 95 percent of the time is going to become more valuable, not less valuable as the years pass. Especially if you follow the methods in this book that teach you to buy property right so you can afford the necessary improvements that will revitalize the neighborhood and make it a better home for residents. All that adds value and it makes sense to ride the wave of appreciation long term.

Myth #4: Some People Just Have the Midas Touch

It is easy to think that people who are successful investing in real estate have some sort of Midas Touch. But there is no such thing. They are just people who see opportunities and know how to make them real and profitable.

Take any ten-acre piece of land. Let's say this parcel is flanked by significant retail presence on all sides and most of the big retail chains are represented in adjacent centers. There's also a large microchip manufacturer nearby that employs 1,000 people.

Ask a tract home builder and he'll see forty single-family homes on that ten acres. Ask a custom builder, and he'll see ten luxury estates. Ask a retail commercial developer and she'll see a new shopping center anchored by two large retailers, with specialty stores and restaurants as fill-in. Ask a multifamily developer and she'll see a 150-unit apartment community with clubhouse, pool, and workout facility. Another commercial developer who specializes in office space may see a three-story office building. In other words, everyone sees the property differently, and each vision will deliver a different level of payout—some better than others.

The important part of recognizing opportunities is common sense. People who seem to have the Midas Touch use their common sense when looking at property and opportunities. In the example here, common sense tells me that building custom homes would be a tough sell on a ten-acre parcel flanked by heavily trafficked retail. Single-family tract homes may be just as challenging. Additional retail may be viable if the developer can lure high-quality anchor tenants to the location. But they may already be operating in other nearby centers. By far in this example, either multi-unit housing or office space are the most viable options. Why? Because of the nearby employment base, the absence of apartments in the area, the proximity to retail, and the lack of office rentals. The developer in this instance who builds offices or apartments will have the best chance of success and will appear to have the Midas Touch. There's no magic, just common sense.

How do you know you're relying on your common sense? It's easy. If everyone you talk with is having difficulty seeing your vision for a property it can be either one of two things: A revolutionary idea that will prove everyone wrong. Or a bad idea that everyone recognizes as a bad idea, except you. In 99 percent of the cases, the latter proves to be true. Remember, if you have to hard-sell your vision for a property to everyone you share it with, it is likely your project when completed will be a hard sell, too! And that will cost you money.

Myth #5: You Need a Great Deal of Confidence

Not true. People underestimate themselves all the time. They listen to that little voice of self-doubt that whispers and sometimes shouts in their brain telling them all the reasons why they can't do something, why they shouldn't even try. I believe there are two voices: the voice of reason, and the voice of self-doubt. The voice of reason is common sense; the voice of self-doubt is your past leading your future.

I made a conscious decision not to let my past dictate my future. I grew up in an average middle-class home. There's nothing wrong with that. In fact, in my estimation, there's everything right with that. I worked for what I got. I learned solid values. A good deal of that came from my parents. My father was not particularly entrepreneurial until later in his career. Hardworking, yes, but not entrepreneurial. He worked for the same company for most of his career and earned a stable living that supported our middle-class lifestyle. It was a good life for me, my brother, and two sisters.

When I got out of college I followed in my dad's footsteps and got a job. But while in that job, I began to meet people—people who showed me their entrepreneurial ways. They became my mentors, and from them I became entrepreneurial. Then I combined the innate values I received from my parents and my own newfound entrepreneurial spirit and I became whole.

Nothing in my upbringing would have prepared me for what I'm doing now. And yet everything did. I believe it is up to each of us to let go of the memories and the scars of unsupportive fathers, ultra-critical mothers, ridiculing friends, and teachers who labeled us from the first day of school. Everybody has had negative influences in their lives and every one of us will have lots more. Look at Hollywood. What's a celebrity profile on E! without the struggles, without the strife? Everyone must rise from challenging situations—that's what successful people do. They decide to get beyond their past, whatever it may be. I've chosen to accept my past, learn from it, copy what was good, and realize the bad stuff only makes me stronger.

Real estate investing is a business where you will need to draw on your strength. My advice is not only to look for strength in all that is good in your life, but also to use the hard times for what they are: character-building experiences. And contrary to what most people think, we can never have enough character. That's my soapbox on confidence and character. The rest of this book is dedicated to building your property investment business.

Myth #6: You Want to Do It but Don't Really Have the Time

This really comes down to choices and priorities. There is always time to do the things we need to do like go to work every day, mow the lawn, feed the dog. Often there isn't time to do the things we really want to do. Learn to speak a second language, build a bookcase, or volunteer in the community. There is a difference between need and want. We'll often do what we need and put off what we want. Unfortunately our wants are what truly enrich our lives.

The investment real estate business is something you should want to do and may even need to do. It's work. To be truly successful, especially in the beginning, you will be involved in the day-to-day activities of finding and evaluating property, negotiating deals, overseeing contract repair work, possibly even managing the property once it's yours. I can honestly say, I find the business rewarding, fun, and because of that, it is profitable.

I fell victim to the myth of not having enough time myself, and I take full blame. Sharon Lechter and Robert Kiyosaki asked me to write this book two years ago. Finally I embraced the idea and actually started wanting to get it done. But wanting was not enough. What got me going was a do-it-or-else deadline. That got my attention and made me realize I needed to get disciplined and write the book. That's what got the book done.

If you don't have the time to begin your real estate investment business, maybe in your mind, you don't really *need* to do it. Maybe you simply *want* to do it, and "want" alone may not be enough to get you started. After all, if you work during the week at another job, you will have to search for and evaluate property on the weekends. You'll need to make phone calls when you can during the week or in the evenings. There's always a way to make your dreams come true . . . as long as they are truly your dreams.

Myth #7: You Have to Know Somebody to Get Going in This Business

While knowing a few key people such as a real estate agent, an attorney, or a banker may save you some time, you don't need to know anyone even remotely connected with investment real estate to get started. In this book, you'll discover the key people you need to have on your team. And you'll find that the goals you set for yourself will actually define the team. People you know today may or may not be the ideal people for your team once you determine what you want to gain from your real estate investment business.

Just get started and you'll be surprised how many people you'll get to know and how much they will teach you. You'll have "friends in the business" before you know it. Here's what I mean. We're doing a deal in Portland, Oregon. I live and work in Arizona. I hadn't been to Portland in over ten years. Anyone I had once known there was long since gone. Neither I nor anyone else in my company knew a soul in Portland. What we did know was that the city was situated on two rivers and that unemployment was high. The latter meant that the people who owned property were probably not doing so well. And to me that spelled buying opportunity. We had one big problem: We knew *about* the city, but we didn't know a single person *in* the city. We figured the market conditions were at least worth a plane trip and a few days in Portland.

Before our trip, we made our minds up to find our team, at least the start of it. So we went on the Internet and looked up property managers, city officials, brokers, and so on in preparation for our trip. We were not about to travel that far and not meet with anyone who could educate us about the market. As a result, we had ten or twelve meetings over a period of two days. It cost us a few lunches and dinners, but we had the beginnings of our team.

Myth #8: You Have to Be a Seasoned Negotiator and Businessperson

Again, this is just not true. Experience in business may make that first walk into an investor's office more comfortable, but that's all it will do. Your true power and confidence won't come from your past experience. Instead, it will come from the solid deal you assemble that is a win-win for everyone involved. This book will show you how to find and evaluate property with the ultimate goal of establishing a realistic purchase price that maximizes your monthly income and appreciates the asset. Find a deal like that and everyone will want a piece of the action.

Over the years, I've walked away from a lot of deals, and negotiation had nothing to do with it. One of those deals was a 205-unit building in Glendale, Arizona. About a year ago the listing price was $7.9 million, and the broker told me there were other offers—the highest one being $7.2 million. We did our homework on the property and by my estimation, $7.2 million was fair based on the operations of the property. The seller declined every offer and pulled the listing. Six months later, the seller relisted the building for $8.1 million. If I had still been interested in the property I would have made an offer based on operations. It would have been the same $7.2 million offer I made before. The seller would probably kick me out, along with everyone else who made him an offer based on operations. Are you surprised to learn that he still owns the building today?

With the method in this book, you'll find out that the listing price is meaningless. There is no point negotiating based on this number, and actually doing so is a recipe for disaster. That's because in most cases, the listing price is the seller's opinion of what the property is worth. It is not founded on the actual operations of the property. What most people consider negotiation meetings are for me more accurately described as presentation meetings. That's when I present the numbers, and they are pretty much take-it-or-leave-it deals. When I get kicked out, and in truth, usually it is a mutual parting of the ways, it's because the numbers don't work. Walking away is a good thing.

Myth #9: You Have to Know a Lot About Real Estate

This myth holds people back every single day. They feel they have to already be experts in a field in order to be successful, whether it is real estate or stock investing or dry cleaning! First of all, success is a journey, it's not a destination, and all successful people start at the same place. One day they wake up, they throw their legs over the side of the bed, they yawn—and they begin.

Only by beginning and by continuing day after day do we ever become experts. We gain expertise through experience. By reading this book, you'll get a solid framework from which to begin. And you'll gain enough knowledge to sound really smart at cocktail parties and backyard barbecues, but more importantly you'll learn tons more from your first deal. And more still from your second and third. And even more from your fourth.

I learn something new with every venture. Some of the buildings we recently bought in Portland were built on an old wooden pier constructed in the 1930s. Who would have guessed when I embarked in this business that I would have to learn everything about the structural integrity of seventy-year-old piers? Not me, but we needed to find out everything about the condition of that pier before we went forward and purchased the property. I live in the desert. So you can imagine how foreign it was for me to hire divers and a boat and structural engineers to do the inspections. It was a real learning experience. I'm always encountering something new. That's part of what keeps it all interesting.

The only way you'll know a lot about real estate is to begin in real estate. Once you do that, you'll meet people, learn your market, see the patterns, and understand the trends. You'll encounter your own seventy-year-old wooden piers, but that will keep it fun. And before you know it, you'll be wowing people at cocktail parties and barbecues with experiences you've lived rather than just read about.

Myth #10 You Can't Be Afraid of Failing

Show me an entrepreneur who says he or she isn't afraid of failing and I'll show you a liar! A bold statement, absolutely, but a true one. Everyone is afraid of failing. The difference is that some of us let that fear of failure hold us back. Sometimes fear stops us from beginning altogether and that's unfortunate. If that's the case, make the decision now to just begin putting one foot in front of the other, making one phone call at a time, visiting one property, and then another. It's not hard, but it can seem so if we focus on the end result instead of the tiny—and very doable—steps in between.

Sometimes fear of failure occurs when it comes time to "pull the trigger" on a property. I call it analysis paralysis and people fall into it all the time. They overanalyze an opportunity and are never quite able to sign on the dotted line. This book will prove especially helpful to people with this sort of fear because it will show you exactly what you need to know to analyze an investment property. When the numbers add up, no further analysis is necessary. Frozen in fear will be a thing of the past.

Another way fear of failure presents itself is through regret. In other words, we've pulled the trigger, but then when difficulties occur—and they will occur, they always do—we regret the decision and waste energy by asking "Why did we do this?" instead of "What can we do to get past the hurdle?" This form of fear can turn an otherwise great opportunity into a bad investment. In my life, I don't regret decisions. I just consider the place where I'm at as the starting line and go for the gold every day.

I admit when I was just starting out I had an acute fear of failing. The difference is I knew that if I did nothing and remained frozen in fear, I would fail. I felt I had a better chance of success by just going forward one step at a time to make some opportunities pay off. That's the thing about fear of failure, if you don't use it to your advantage as a motivator, it becomes a self-fulfilling prophecy.

Myth #11: You Have to Know the Tricks of the Trade

There are no tricks of the trade in the purest sense of the term. But there are secrets to success in life. And as long as you know those, you'll be successful at anything. First, you have to set goals. Goals will be the foundation of the roadmap for your success. They will also tell you when you have arrived, so you can pat yourself on the back. Everyone needs that reinforcement. Not coincidentally the next chapter is all about goal setting.

Second, you have to persevere. Quitting when things get tough doesn't produce winners. In fifteen years, I could have quit a hundred times. I've had plenty of tough problems. Financing that falls through, employee problems, and downright frightening resident issues. But successful people work through difficulties and they come out on the other side stronger, more confident, and better prepared for the next challenge. And trust me, there will be more challenges.

Finally, you have to understand the process. That's what this book will do. It will take you from beginning to end and every step in between. From setting goals to setting up your team, to finding property, to evaluating it, to determining a purchase price, to managing it, I'll let you in on fifteen years' worth of experience. I hope this book will become your handbook for success.

═══════ CHAPTER 1 ACTION STEPS ═══════

- Understand the myths in this chapter.

- Ask yourself if there are any others.

- Identify the ones you believe to be true.

- Determine which myths have been responsible for hindering your success.

- Make the commitment to abandon these unproductive myths.

- Make the commitment to learn techniques and preparedness so magical things happen.

Chapter 2

You Gotta Have a Goal

The title of this chapter spells out pretty clearly how I feel about goals and real estate investment. Having a goal is not optional. Goal setting is step number one in the process. In this chapter, you'll learn how to set your goal, what a realistic goal should look like, and set milestones to achieve it. You'll come to understand the benefits of goal setting and discover how "goal power" can be your key to success.

When I first started out, I had a goal. I wanted to be my own boss. I was tired of working for someone else, and wanted to start some sort of business on my own. Admittedly, I never actually wrote down my goal in those early days, and I didn't tell too many people either. In fact I barely verbalized it to myself. More accurately, I felt it.

It wasn't until years later that I really understood goal power, the power you feel when you've set a target and you concentrate all your efforts on hitting it. It makes you focused. It makes you decisive. And ultimately it makes you successful. I don't know if anyone else before me has used the term "goal power." It just seemed to accurately communicate a fact that's important right now: that having a goal makes you powerful.

What's a Goal?

It's easy to get hung up on terminology. Is that a goal? Is it a vision? Maybe it's an objective? Maybe it's a mission? Forget all that right now. And don't worry about textbook definitions. My goal with this book is for it to become the best-selling guide that simplifies the process of real estate investing by showing you how to find, buy, and manage property right, and I may as well start with goal setting.

A GOAL IS SOMETHING YOU PLAN TO ACHIEVE

Simply stated, a goal is something you plan to achieve. Maybe your goal is to buy one investment property in a twelve-month period. Or maybe you want to earn $5,000 per month in income within two years. You might even set your goal so high that you decide you want to be the number one rental property owner in your town within five years.

Whatever goal you set, make sure it is something you plan to achieve. Nothing is more valueless than a goal that sits on a shelf and never receives any action. Those are simply dreams. There's no real power in dreams unless they are acted upon.

YOUR GOAL SHOULD BE MEASURABLE

Your goal should be measurable. My goal of wanting to be my own boss wasn't really a good goal. As I said, it took me years to learn how to set goals and to take advantage of the power they harness. A much better goal for me would have included a time limit, say within one year, to become my own boss, or an earnings level, like earning $75,000 per year.

Goals that are vague are hard to attain and are even harder to stick to. If there is no time limit, dollar amount, or rank comparison, for example, how will you know you have "arrived"? It's virtually impossible.

One real estate investor I know has a very measurable goal to acquire one two-unit property per year. Another has a goal of acquiring ten homes a year. The point here is that the goals are achievable and measurable. What will your goal be?

YOUR GOAL SHOULD BE ATTAINABLE

Goals must be realistic and attainable, otherwise they will either be shelved and never acted upon or modified midstream to something more realistic. The latter alternative is acceptable, but goals that are set too high can trigger feelings of failure if not attained. On the other hand, they can be exhilarating if actually achieved.

My first goal of becoming my own boss was very achievable looking back on it. But at the time it seemed like an ambitious dream. After all, I had a steady job that paid for my car, my house, my lifestyle. Deciding to give all that up was frightening, but I knew it was something I had to do. The goal, while lofty, was not impossible. And that gave me hope, motivation, and a desire to achieve it.

Setting Your Goal

Goal setting requires you to be honest with yourself and reflect on what you really want in life. That means taking the time to think about what you want for yourself and your family right now, in the years ahead, and long into the future. It may even include aspirations you have for your children. If you think this level of goal setting is a waste of time, you may want to reconsider.

I learned about two fantastic goal setting programs through my involvement in an association called Young Entrepreneurs' Organization (YEO). I'm part of the Arizona chapter and my involvement has been one of the best business decisions I've made in my career.

The first program is called Strategic Coach, and it's founded and run by Dan Sullivan. This program is centered on the "seven laws" for experiencing continued personal growth and helping you develop a life plan. Strategic Coach meets with you every quarter to see how you are doing to achieve your goal.

The Strategic Coach Seven Laws of Lifetime Growth:

1. Always make your future better than your past.
2. Always make your contribution bigger than your reward.
3. Always make your learning greater than your experience.
4. Always make your performance greater than your applause.
5. Always make your gratitude greater than your success.
6. Always make your enjoyment greater than your effort.
7. Always make your confidence greater than your comfort.

There's another terrific program called Setting Family Goals by Charlie and Barbara Dunlap. This program focuses on balancing your marriage, family, and business. Think about it, how much time do you spend planning your workday? How much time do you spend planning your family or your marriage? If you were like me, planning work was at the top of the list and I spent very little time planning my family goals.

After meeting with Charlie and Barbara Dunlap, I now have a solid plan for my marriage, my family, and my work. Work is now in third position, behind marriage and family. Once I developed a marriage and a family plan, I actually became a better businessperson because my personal goals integrated with my work goals.

Charlie and Barbara say your goals should be general, but it is the specific to do's and the objectives that need to pass the SMART test.

"S" specific
"M" measurable
"A" agreed upon in writing
"R" realistic
"T" time activated

Charlie also happens to be my personal mentor and I meet him once a month. Strategic Coach, Charlie and Barbara Dunlap, and a host of other similar organizations enroll thousands into their programs every year. People are setting goals and shaping their lives . . . intentionally. If you think this is crazy, know there are whole industries built on this, and people everywhere are using goal setting to make their dreams realities.

It's been said "a goal not written down is a wish." I've also heard "a goal is nothing more than a dream without a time limit." I made a decision a long time ago not to risk my future on wishes and dreams. Instead I got smart and set goals with the help of people like Charlie and Barbara. You can reach Setting Family Goals at ChadDunCo@aol.com.

These are the people who are setting courses for their lives and living them. Sure there will be bumps in the road and sometimes they will get off course—even change their courses purposely along the way. But the bottom line is that their goals empower them.

YOUR GOAL MAY EVOLVE OVER TIME

After a few years of working for myself as one of the two principal owners in Arizona-based MC Companies, the real estate investment firm my partner and I still own today, I began to discover that my goal had evolved. I wanted to be more than just my own boss. I realized that I wanted freedom. Freedom financially to do the things in life I wanted to do. Like spend time with my children. Coach Little League and travel with my family. I knew this goal could only be attained through the accumulation of wealth, wealth that would appreciate over time. So my partner and I, in addition to managing properties, began investing in them as well. Today, I have a measurable goal related to financial freedom. I'm not there yet, but I'm working on it!

There's nothing wrong with a goal that evolves over time, unless you are changing your goal every time you hit a roadblock. That's called avoidance. Over time as you are working to achieve your goal, your experiences will make you smarter. You may even see things a whole new way. Your goal may shift as a result of new awareness. My first goal was to be my own boss. That evolved into a goal of financial freedom, and now my goal is to help others who want to do the same.

MAKE YOURSELF ACCOUNTABLE TO SOMEBODY

When I set a goal for myself a few years ago to get back in shape, I knew I'd have a better chance of succeeding if I had a partner. You know, someone who I'd meet at the gym every morning. Someone who would egg me on to do just one more set on the bench press machine. Someone who I knew, on those mornings when I just didn't feel like running, would be waiting for me up the road at 5:30. This is accountability and goals are easier to attain when there are one or more people supporting and encouraging you.

At MC Companies I have my partner, Ross McCallister. Ross and I help each other stay on course with our five-year strategic plan. We also share the plan with the entire company of over 150 employees. By including everyone in the vision everyone knows how they fit in. We're also accountable to one another, and we're all working in the same direction.

The person or persons you are accountable to could be a business associate, a friend, your husband or wife, even your investors and employees. The important thing is to find a person who is encouraging and supportive of your venture. That's not to say you're looking for a person who never challenges your decisions. On the contrary, you're looking for a person who is based in reality and supportive of your dream.

Achieving Your Goal

Setting your goal is certainly an important first step, but what you do after that really defines the level of success you will ultimately achieve. Achieving my goals meant I had to do four things really well: Communicate, plan, persevere, and stay focused. Let's look at these important concepts in more detail.

COMMUNICATE YOUR GOAL CLEARLY

If you have goal fear, that is the fear of telling anyone your goal in case you don't achieve it, get beyond it. When you have your goal set on paper and burned into your psyche, tell everyone. Tell your real estate agent, tell your attorney, tell your friends, family members, business associates, I mean everyone. These are the people who will help you attain it. And in case I haven't made it clear yet, goals are never achieved alone.

Here's an example of a hypothetical goal:

> We will acquire one eight-unit property in the Phoenix metro area within the next twelve months that will generate at least $4,000 of average annual income over the next five years.

That's a goal. It's measurable and it's clearly defined. It's certainly attainable. All that is really left is to make it happen. Contrast that goal with this uninspired and nonmotivating goal statement:

> I want to invest in some real estate and am looking for a good rental property deal that will supplement my income.

This goal is extremely vague. It's hard to realistically attain and difficult to execute. And forget about communicating it! But unfortunately, that's how most people set and communicate goals, if you can call this statement a goal. It really sounds more like a pipe dream.

If you share a goal as written in the first example with a few real estate agents, a few mortgage brokers, and some property managers, I know you will get calls. They will bring you opportunities because they can tell you are serious, that you know what you want, and that you have a set time limit. If you go to the same group with the goal as written in the second example, they will probably not respond at all because they don't know how. There's nothing there for them to sink their teeth into. Few if any opportunities will come to you; instead, you'll be forced to find opportunities yourself. And given the vagueness of the goal, you have a lot of work ahead of you.

Communicating a goal effectively puts you in the driver's seat. In the first goal example, you're in charge. In the second goal example, if any real estate agents respond to you, they will be showing you the properties that are in *their* interest to sell, not necessarily in *your* best interest to buy. That's a dangerous position.

You'll know whether or not your goals are concrete by listening to what you say. Should you find yourself saying phrases like, "If you hear of anything, let me know . . ." or "Tell me if you see anything that looks good . . ." then you need to define your goal further. Those phrases are telltale signs of vagueness.

PLAN AND SET MILESTONES

Once you have your clear, measurable goal defined, you'll also want to lay out the path you plan to take to achieve it. That means drafting a plan and setting milestones so you know when you've achieved important steps along the way.

There are fundamental milestones that relate to personal behaviors and financial freedom.

What behaviors should we change or eliminate?

Behavioral Change to Do List

Taking the same route to work every day

Hour-long lunches

Watching TV every night

By changing these three simple behaviors you are setting milestones that help you achieve your goal. Taking a different route to work gives you new scenery and helps you learn about the market and the properties within it. It helps you understand traffic patterns and gives you new perspective on new areas. Using half your lunch hour to eat frees up the other half to make phone calls, meet with your team, and even visit properties. And in case you're a numbers person, a half-hour per weekday adds up to ten hours per month! Finally, eliminating TV, or at least reducing your viewing time, frees up countless hours in the evenings to work on your business. Look at your own behaviors and modify them to achieve your goals.

How much money do you need to make to be financially free and what are you going to do to make it happen?

Financial Freedom to Do List

Add up your personal expenses

Determine what you can reduce, eliminate, or do without

Figure out how many properties you need to buy to cover the total

Over the years I've established a system that I use every time. It's the system you'll discover in this book. You should also communicate milestones clearly to your network of business partners, and everyone you meet. You never know who will be the one to reveal the perfect property opportunity to you, so the more detail you can provide up front the better.

Business to Do List

Find your team

Evaluate the market

Find a great property

Assign a valuation to the property

Establish a property plan

Develop a budget

Manage the property

Use the chart to help you map out your goals. Be honest with yourself and write in those things that you really plan to accomplish.

PERSEVERE AND DRIVE THROUGH ALL OBSTACLES

If you've ever been part of anything entrepreneurial or even if you ever built something from scratch, then you know endeavors such as these take twice as long as you think, require twice as much work, and cost a lot more than you expected. Those are facts of life, so I am never surprised when they prove to be true. Every project brings with it obstacles. Things that make work work, if you want to look at it that way. Or, things that keep work interesting. I prefer the latter.

In Portland, the acquisition of our waterfront building is destined to be a great investment. It's right on the Willamette River, and as I mentioned earlier, part of the building is built on the pier. There are waterfront views and the entire project is over 300 units. There's nothing else like it in the whole city. Sounds like a dream come true. Well many would have viewed the dream more like a nightmare from the start. From problems stemming from years of deferred maintenance to battling numerous structural inadequacies, you name it and we encountered it. We could have let these obstacles and dozens of others stop us a hundred times from closing on this deal. But we knew in our hearts this property was worth the effort. It was worth driving through every one of these obstacles. We found solutions and invested the money necessary to bring this amazing project to its full potential.

When it comes to property investing,
the saying "where there's a will,
there's a way" has never been
more meaningful.

KEEP YOUR FOCUS

There's a funny thing about goals and success. The closer you get to achieving your goal and the more successful you become, the more opportunities will come your way. You'll be tempted on almost a weekly basis with new properties and other business opportunities that promise to increase your revenue. The "sure things" will come out of the woodwork.

At least this is how it was and still is for me. All these opportunities are great, but you can't let them steer you away from your goal. Here's what happened to me. After we had built our property management business to a significant size and had begun looking for ways to increase revenue, I decided to start a carpet cleaning company. It made sense at the time; after all, we had thousands of apartment units with carpets to clean, why should that business go to some other company? That single lesson cost me a quarter of a million dollars. But even more than the money, it took my eye off my goal for at least a year or two. It slowed the pace of our growth. Our company would have achieved its goal a lot quicker if it hadn't been for this diversion. I guess I should say I learned more than one lesson on that deal.

As opportunities present themselves, ask yourself, "How many balls do I want to juggle? If I take on this project can I manage ten more balls in the air? And more importantly, will taking on this project get me closer to achieving my goal?" If your goal is to buy an eight-unit property and earn an average of $4,000 per year in the next five years, will a hot deal on a single-family home get you closer to achieving that? No it won't, and in fact, it will divert your attention from the original goal and certainly not net you $4,000 per year in income over the next five years. If you are set on your goal—and you should be—sometimes it means passing up great deals that don't support it. Focus equals discipline.

Goal setting is not an option; it is a requirement for success. The sooner you begin establishing your goal, the sooner you'll be ready to take the next step—establishing your team.

CHAPTER 2 ACTION STEPS

- Understand and believe in goal power as a means to accomplish your dreams.

- Search within yourself and set a goal for your real estate investment business.

- Overcome goal fear, which is the fear of telling others your goal in case you fail.

- Find someone to whom you can be accountable.

- Tell everyone you see about your goal.

- Set milestones, the baby steps, for achieving your goal.

- Tell everyone about your milestones.

Chapter 3

It Takes a Team

Who was it that said "No man is an island"? Whoever he was, he could have been living in the twenty-first century because today we don't do anything without the help of other people. Even when movie stars win Academy Awards, they never walk up to the podium, face the crowd, smile, and say, "Thank you. I am quite wonderful for having done this all by myself." Instead, it practically takes a vaudeville cane to yank them off the stage as they thank the hundreds of people who helped them all along the way. Everyone has a team. Even the Lone Ranger had Tonto and Silver!

Well, in the business of investment real estate, you can't afford to be a lone ranger. In fact, it's impossible to accomplish your goal on your own no matter what your goal is. And no one is expecting you to. Quite the opposite. We're expecting you to build an extensive network and a close-knit team that will be your most valuable resource.

Why Have a Team?

Having a team of experts on call is not free and it is not cheap. Those are the two biggest reasons why many inexperienced investors make a rookie mistake: They try to do almost everything themselves. Sure, they may save a few dollars in the short run, but they usually lose in the long run. Without experts on your team, deals take longer to find, evaluate, and close, so there's the value of your time and the loss of valuable opportunities. Do-it-yourselfers miss details that experts would see in a minute, like clauses missing in contracts, obvious defects in construction, and hundreds if not thousands of other issues experts would point out up front.

An expert team on your side means you'll have fewer surprises as you wade through the sometimes turbulent waters of purchasing and managing a property. Surprises are wonderful on birthdays, but the kinds of surprises that come from investment property are usually not very welcome.

Real-World Case

One investor who decided to go it alone is a man from Seattle who called us right after he purchased a 100-unit property and asked us to help him manage it. The key word here is "after." The property is in Phoenix and he had absolutely no plan for it. He had never walked into any of the units; he never called anyone to inquire what the resident mix was like. He never even checked what kind of neighborhood the property was in. When we talked it was obvious he had not done any research at all on the property; he bought it sight unseen. The property was in massive disrepair—a nice way of saying it should have been condemned—and worse than that, it was full of gang members. Even the Phoenix police department was instructed to never enter the premises without backup.

This man's laziness on the front end cost him tons of money. I wonder why now, but we did take on the management contract for this property and the price tag was pretty steep to get this place back in shape. Outside contractors of every kind, lawyers, you name it, we hired them all. We sent eviction notices that nearly evacuated the entire place just to get rid of the riffraff. That meant the owner endured months of significantly reduced income and sky-high marketing costs to get the property leased. It was a mess that took the better part of a year. If this man had taken the time to establish a network of people in Phoenix before buying property, they would have either steered him clear of this property or flushed out all the issues so he could have established a plan to turn the property around.

This is just one example. There are thousands of others. The point here is simply that the wise investor pays on the front end and reaps the rewards on the back end. The fees it would have cost the property owner from Seattle to have his Phoenix team visit the property and file a report or two were a pittance when compared with what it cost him out of his own pocket to get his investment in shape. Had the work been identified up front, the cost of the property improvements would have been factored into the seller's listing price. Build your team now. You'll save money and be prepared for whatever you encounter along the way.

And here's one more bonus. Often it is the team you establish that becomes the foundation for your entire network. Think of your network as your lifeline. Not only will they help you with the deals you're working on now, they are usually the ones who will bring you your second, third, and fourth property opportunities—particularly if you have voiced your goal to them clearly, as discussed in the previous chapter. There's no need to do all the work yourself. You need experts. I've been doing this for years and I still rely on my team of experts. I wouldn't do a deal without them.

My Brother-in-Law Is an Accountant

People have wildly different views on partnering with family members. Some say go for it and save a bundle. Others say avoid it at all costs. I fall somewhere in between. I believe that having family members on your team, or even partnering with them, is a good idea as long as you make an informed decision and know what you are getting into. You'll want to go in with your eyes wide open on this one, because, let's face it, next year's Thanksgiving dinner is on the line. Plenty of families can mix business relationships with personal relationships and do just fine. Others have not mastered the art. Only you know where your family fits in.

Having family members on your team has some pros and cons as you can see in the table below:

The Pros and Cons of Working with Family Members

Pros:

- It's easy. This is definitely the easy way. If my brother-in-law is an accountant, I have that chore done. No need to spend time shopping around.

- Keeps the peace. In some families, hostilities may occur if you *don't* use the in-house pro.

- Low cost or no cost. Often family members will give away their services to relatives for nothing.

Cons:

- Loss of objectivity. It's hard to have the tough conversations you need in business with a family member and still "pass the turkey" the next day.

- Loss of bargaining power. I evaluate rates and fee annually with all my suppliers; this is tough to do with family members.

- Loss of relationships. Families have been destroyed over bad business dealings.

Whichever route you choose—to employ the talents of family members, or to not employ them—know that your degree of success will be directly proportional to your degree of integrity. People like to work with fair and honest people. This book and its methods are based on those values. Master them and I guarantee you'll sleep better at night and not surprisingly, people will line up to work with you.

Partners—A Good Thing or a Bad Idea

At MC Companies my partner, Ross, and I have been together since almost day one. His skills and my skills dovetail perfectly. He handles the construction and development and I handle the management and operations. We both handle acquisitions and together we each bring to the deal our own unique perspectives. It's a great relationship and because we have mutual respect and honesty, it works. We also push each other along, as I recommended in the last chapter. It's great to have someone to whom you are accountable. We've accomplished a lot more together than we ever would have accomplished alone.

QUALITIES OF A GOOD PARTNERSHIP

Some partnerships are destined for success and others are doomed to failure right from the start. What makes or breaks a partnership? Here are some qualities good partnerships have in common:

- Healthy debate: You should have room for debate before decisions are made.

- Open-mindedness: You shouldn't have to spend valuable time continually convincing your partner of your goals.

- Commitment: You should be committed to each other and your goals.

- Similar values: You and your partner should share the same values.

- Accountability: You and your partner should push each other to achieve objectives and have mutual accountability.

These qualities will guide you in establishing a partnership in your business. Now we'll look at how to partner with others outside your company: setting up your team.

Your All-Important Team

The following lists include all the people and professionals you will eventually have on your team and how to evaluate and select them. While the lists may appear overwhelming, understand that you will accumulate these contacts over time, and you don't need all of them at all times. There's no need to run out and start interviewing paving companies, for example, when you don't have a parking lot that needs resurfacing. You just need a few key team members to get started—an attorney, an accountant, a real estate broker, and a property manager. But here are the full lists to get you prepared:

YOUR BUSINESS TEAM

Before you do anything, even print your business cards and letter-head, get your business set up correctly. To do that you'll need to talk with an attorney who will advise you about setting up your company. Should you set up a corporation, a limited liability company, or some other business entity? You'll need to know the pros and cons of each to make that decision. Regardless of which you choose, having a formal company established will protect your personal assets and provide tax advantages to you. If you need more information before choosing your own business team, you should contact:

• Your own attorney. You'll need this person to file the paperwork with the corporation commission. There are do-it-yourself kits, but unless you know what you're doing, I advise against them.

• Your own accountant. This person will be able to give you tax advice based on your own personal financial situation.

THE PROPERTY SEARCH TEAM

The property search team includes people you will most likely have to find on your own. I recommend interviewing several professionals in each field until you find people you like, who know the market, have your same level of integrity, and who understand they are there to help you achieve your goal. Both of these professionals can also help you establish the rest of your team especially for the property inspections commonly called due diligence once you get into escrow.

- Real estate broker. The real estate broker will help you understand your market and help you find properties.
- Property manager. This person will help you assess the properties you are considering from an operational perspective. They will give you a solid idea of what you are getting into.

THE OFFER TEAM

Your property search team will most likely refer some or all of these professionals to you as you need them. That's another reason why who you choose as your real estate broker and your property management contacts are so critical. They set the tone for your entire team and therefore your entire work experience. Choose wisely!

- Attorney. Your attorney will certainly help you set up your business, but he or she will also help you wade through letters of intent and purchase and sale agreements.
- Lender or mortgage broker. Find a lender or broker who understands the business of property investing. Not only will they lend

you money, but they will also provide you with leads on other properties that are ripe for sale.

• Investors. By communicating your goals and doing the work of building your team, you should find several sources of equity who will entertain investing in rental property.

• Contractor/Rehab specialist. Contractors see things you and I don't when it comes to walking a property. Before I sign any deal, I have a contractor perform a detailed inspection and file a report of all critical and noncritical repairs.

OTHER TEAM MEMBERS

From time to time, you may find you need these professionals to assist with projects that arise when either considering a property or once you own it. As with the professionals on the previous list, these team members will come to you through referrals.

• Accountant. Your accountant will help you not only with your own business finances, but also help you put together profit-and-loss projections for the properties you are considering.

• Appraiser. An appraiser is an important team member and should be a person who specializes in both your market and the types of properties you are targeting. This professional will help you determine the appraised value of property before and after the sale.

• Architect. Some properties need more than just a coat of paint and the bushes trimmed to get them into shape. An architect can help you with new design ideas and renovations to increase curb appeal and operations performance.

• Insurance agent. The insurance agent will help you place the proper protections when you own the property. Having the right coverage for the right price will be necessary if you acquire property.

• Property tax consultant. Property taxes are realities in this business and property tax consultants can ensure that your taxes are being assessed fairly and accurately.

• Income tax consultant. The tax laws are complicated and it is always good to have the advice of someone whose job it is to keep up with tax law.

• Estate planner. As your real estate assets grow, an estate planner can help you shelter and dispose of them in the event of illness or death.

• Environmental company/industrial hygienist. If you suspect mold, asbestos, or any other environmental hazard, you'll need one of these to help you through the process of testing and removal if necessary.

• Surveyor. As you are rehabilitating a property, you may need the services of a surveyor to assess boundary lines, elevations, and other such matters.

• Structural engineer. Your contractor may find a problem that jeopardizes the structural integrity of the building. Call in a structural engineer, who will analyze the problem and recommend a strategy to repair the building.

Teams are just that: People who work together to get the job done. They should be on your side and have the mentality that when you are successful, they are successful. Keep searching until you find people whose goals and business methods gel with your own.

═══ CHAPTER 3 ACTION STEPS ═══

- Understand it takes a team to be successful in this business.

- Determine whether you want a partner.

- Evaluate partner candidates based on the qualities of a good partnership.

- Establish your business team first—an attorney and an accountant.

- Begin networking to find other team members for your property search team, your offer team, and other team members you'll need from time to time.

Chapter 4

Research Can Be Fun?

At Robert Kiyosaki's Rich Dad Seminars where I often speak, attendees always ask me, "How do I find good investment property?" This has to be the most commonly asked question, and for good reason. There is a needle-in-a-haystack sort of quality to this whole endeavor, or at least it seems that way, particularly if you've never done it before. Do you look in the newspaper, grab sales sheets from real estate offices, check out the Internet, drive around? The whole thing seems so haphazard. Truth be told, there is a lot of information out there about property and a lot of ways to get that information. Maybe too many ways. Knowing which resources are valuable and knowing how to access them can save you time and frustration.

In this chapter, I'll reveal a research strategy that you simply cannot do without. By walking you through my experience of buying a property in a new market I knew nothing about, you'll see how this research method works and what you can gain from it. There's no real trick to this at all. It's just having fun, being open to the information that's available about your market, knowing where to look, and committing yourself to do it.

Researching a market can be a lot like doing the preliminary research for a college paper. Maybe you remember the feeling of stepping into the library for the first time. Looking around at all the books, magazines, computer databases, and microfilm (if you're as old as me) was overwhelming. You knew the information you were looking for was in there somewhere; the problem was finding it and making sense out of it. Your first paper was always the hardest. But once you got familiar with the best sources in the library the next papers get easier and easier. (Well, at least that was what I was told.) My college professors would be proud of me today, because I did eventually learn how to do research. And I learned how to make it really fun. We have a great time researching markets and properties because research to me is nothing more than using the resources around you to gain information and insight into a particular subject. In this business that means talking to people, touring an area, taking in the sights, even within your own town. Kind of sounds like a purposeful, tax-deductible vacation, doesn't it. Well it can be, so let's get the party started!

The research techniques described in this chapter will help you three ways. First, they will give you a snapshot of the various markets and submarkets within your city or town. The more diligent you are about doing the research the more vivid the picture will be. And in the chapters ahead you'll see why a very vivid picture here will save you time and money later. Second, this research will show you how the market will influence your property investment. And third, you actually may be lucky enough to find property leads during the research phase (but don't count on it). The most important fruit from your efforts is the picture of the market. The properties will come later.

I grouped the research I do into three easy-to-define and easily understood categories. The descriptions for each are in the sections that follow.

Level One Research

Level One Research is what I call the very preliminary stuff. To do it, you don't even have to leave your house. This is research you do before you even set foot on a property, or in the case of the true story of our acquisition of the waterfront property in Portland, Oregon, before we even set foot in the town. You should know we didn't just pick Portland out of a hat. Before we settled on Portland, our goal was to do Level One Research on all the major markets in the Western United States. It was time to expand our company's reach, and the question was where to go. One of the first things we did was look at all the newspapers and business journal newspapers in every major Western city via the Internet. We followed the online hyperlinks to every interesting lead.

For example, we'd type in a city like Denver into a search engine and up would pop a story about population growth. We'd follow it. Then as part of that story there'd be a link about school funding. We'd follow it. What we found was very interesting, particularly in Portland. First we discovered that the city has an urban growth boundary that we felt would limit the supply of rental property in the future. That's a good thing! Next we found that the city of Portland was progressive in their downtown planning and progressive in terms of transportation with their light rail, bus system, taxi system, streetcar system, and even plans for a future water taxi on the Willamette River. We also found that living and working downtown was in high demand and that the downtown employment picture was favorable. We were beginning to get our picture of the market. It was looking good.

Then we started to uncover some of the city's limitations. On the downside we found statewide unemployment was leading the country with a whopping 8.1 percent. This was an important finding because when we saw that statewide number compared to unemployment in downtown Portland, we knew for us the only opportunity was downtown or possibly a few other suburban bright spots. Furthermore, downtown was mostly all built out and had even greater supply restrictions than the rest of the metro area. Our job was not going to be easy.

We found out this information in less than a day all from my desk in Phoenix, Arizona. Although there were some negatives about the market, overall we were pleasantly surprised and impressed with Portland. It was nothing like we expected it to be. We thought it would be a place with major corporate layoffs, a place plagued by downturns in the logging industry and agriculture, and one that was especially hard hit by other economic woes including declines in the stock market and the after-effects of the 9/11 tragedy, which had happened just four months earlier. Our preconception of the area was based on the broad brushstrokes painted by the media and, boy, were we wrong.

We saw Portland as a progressive city that was concerned about the quality of life and that had long-term plans for building a wonderful community for today and tomorrow. We also found that downtown Portland was one of the least affordable places to live in the Northwest.

Portland was a mixed bag, but the negatives didn't scare us. In real estate, you've heard the saying buy low and sell high. In most cases the opportunities to buy low are when the economy is down and the press is making a living by saying bad things about you. That was Portland.

The point here is not to sell you on Portland, but to tell you that we would have never known any of this unless we decided to do Level One Research in that area. We would have never found out that downtown Portland was a market with good employment, that it was progressive and forward-thinking, that it had a very high cost of home ownership, and that it was in high demand. This was all good news for rental property investment, contrary to the picture the media painted.

We knew it was worthy of a site visit.

Level Two Research

In Portland, we were a couple of desert dwellers from Arizona who came armed with information but hadn't seen rain in months let alone trees that actually bear leaves. We were as green as the Portland landscape. We plunked right into this market knowing no one. We were prepared, however, to conduct Level Two Research once we got there to develop a team that would help us understand the market and maybe even lead us to property. Research plays an important role in establishing yourself within the market and finding the people who will help you make things happen.

Level Two Research is about meeting face-to-face and we didn't waste time. Even before we arrived we had made phone calls to set up meetings with property managers, commercial brokers, commercial lenders, city officials, and businesspeople like the publisher of the local apartment guide. When we arrived we met with each of them. First of all, they were amazed at how much we knew about the area and the depth of our knowledge. They affirmed the things we presumed to be true and set us straight on the assumptions that were off base. For instance, they confirmed our assumption that the limited supply of housing in downtown Portland was greater than in any other area of the city. They confirmed that there was a high demand to live and work in the city. They confirmed that the downtown area was not only a vibrant, progressive community for those who lived there, but that it was also a draw for people who lived elsewhere through its Saturday markets, jazz festivals, holiday events, convention center, Rose Garden, parades, and more. It was a true city center.

We didn't get everything right during our Level One Research, though. The people we met with surprised us by painting a gloomier picture of the outlying suburban areas than we had painted ourselves. There was more overbuilding than we had assumed and there was more available land than we had assumed. Nike and Intel had a very large presence there without much other employment of any size. The overall picture was clearly a risky one.

It was during this time that we really started narrowing in on our submarket. In any economic downturn, it's always smart to be in the market that will turn positive first. That's true of anything in business whether it's the stock market, a business sector, or real estate. So we looked at several submarkets and determined that downtown Portland was strongest at this point and would be the first to rebound based on the simple economics of supply and demand, its diversified employment base, and lack of affordable housing. We learned that as the economy rebounded, the downtown market would be the area that rebounded first.

While we were meeting with all our contacts, we clearly communicated our goal—to buy a 200-plus-unit apartment community—and asked them a variety of questions like: who their favorite property management people were, what lawyer they recommended for legal work, if they knew any good accountants. We asked for recommendations for every team member we listed in the last chapter. By the time we left two days later, we had a vivid picture of the market, and we had narrowed our search to a viable submarket. We had some good leads for our team, and we were told of several properties that were possibilities. We also took in the sights, ate wonderful dinners, and generally enjoyed our time in Portland.

Level Three Research

When we returned to Arizona, we not only vividly remembered what green trees looked like, we knew Portland was an investment opportunity. But we still needed a bit more information to feel good about making a move there. That's where Level Three Research came into play. We first called every team referral and asked them all the same questions we asked of our initial contacts in Portland. Not only did they give us their opinion and insights, they pointed us in the direction of numerous Web sites, analyst newsletters, economic development offices, city government contacts, and other Portland businesspeople who could add the finishing touches to our picture of Portland and could keep us on top of happenings in the area for as long as necessary. Through this exercise we started to discover who should be on our team.

We signed up for free online newsletters, got on the mailing lists and e-mail lists of real estate agents, commercial brokers, loan officers, and other professionals helpful to us. We are forever in the know and hooked into the network. No longer do we have to seek out all the information, a lot of it comes automatically to us.

During this whole process we felt like detectives following up on leads and putting the evidence together to arrive at a conclusion. By involving others, we were able to maintain our objectivity and keep our perspective. All this took was some time on our part. The biggest out-of-pocket costs were our economy seats on Alaska Airlines and one night at 5th Avenue Suites. We're talking shoestring. And best of all, we paid nothing for the information we received during the process. On top of it all, it was a good time. Why wouldn't you do this?

Ultimately, our vision of an apartment community evolved into a condominium conversion project. The research we did took our vision of an ordinary project and made it extraordinary. We were able to redevelop an area, deliver exactly what the area needed, and give the city and the people what they wanted.

I don't buy anything without researching the market first. Even in Phoenix, which is a market I know extremely well, I do research before I buy anything. Things change, markets and submarkets go in and out of favor, big projects like highways change the patterns and flow of a city. There is always something.

Today, thanks to the Internet, research is easy and takes virtually no time. Everything is online and available. For as difficult as researching that first college term paper was, this is a breeze. And there's never been more riding on getting an A.

CHAPTER 4 ACTION STEPS

- Become familiar with the resources available online like:

  - newspapers
  - business trade publications
  - government Web sites
  - trade organizations

- Realize that government officials and staff people work for you and that meeting with you is part of their job.

- Test your research abilities—see how much information you can find out about your hometown:

  - online
  - through face-to-face meetings
  - through in-depth follow-up phone calls

Chapter 5

Swampland for Sale

Next time you drive to work, take your son or daughter to school, or race down a highway you've traveled hundreds of times, look to the right and the left. Maybe I should say glance. Repeatedly. (It's safer that way.) But what I mean is this: Take the time to really look around. I travel roads, the same ones every day, just like you do. I think I know the area. You probably think you do too. After all, you pass by the same houses, the same stores, the same apartment buildings, the same office parks every day, right? Well, caution here. This type of complacent "knowledge," the knowledge you get by passing by, can be dangerous when it comes to property investing. First impressions and outward appearances of cities or towns and the neighborhoods within them—also called markets and submarkets—can be deceiving.

So can buying anything in a market that you know nothing about. You've heard the saying, and it's true, a lot of swampland gets sold to unsuspecting buyers not just in Florida but in every city and town across America. Every town has its swampland. You know, it's the investment that sucks up all your resources and offers nothing in return. And let's face it, getting people to venture into the murky water is a lot more challenging with alligators lurking around.

If we learn anything from all those poor people who have purchased swampland with the hopes of striking it rich, we should take away one lesson:

> *The market is more important*
> *than the property.*

I'm always amazed by how much there is to know about a specific market or even a small submarket just a few blocks in size. What you see on the surface is just the beginning. And just when I think I know an area really well, something changes. In this chapter, I'll show you how to get beyond the appearances, avoid the swamps, and see the true picture of a market and its smaller submarkets. And in the process you'll gain objectivity—a very good thing indeed when it comes to real estate investing.

The Problem with Gut Feelings

Too many people purchase investment real estate on a hunch or a gut feeling. And while it is important to have instincts, understand that they are the products of experience, not a right of birth. This gets back to the myths. People are not born knowing this stuff. I believe it is impossible for a person who has never done a single investment deal to have an instinctive knowledge that one deal will be better than another. It's not that simple. In fact that's the kind of naive thinking that gets investors off to the wrong start.

Save your gut instincts for twenty years down the road. Starting off on the right foot involves doing one thing really well: evaluating your market and submarket. You must get to know your target area and become an expert in it. Not for the sake of merely being an expert, but for the ultimate purpose of finding a great property investment that is viable and profitable for the long term. That's what we're shooting for here. If you can accomplish that, the rest becomes easy. And that goes for finding and keeping residents, which directly impacts your cash flow and profitability.

I've been in business for a long time and even I don't rely on instincts alone. Before we invested in the Portland River District, we did our homework. You read about our online research, our site visit, our marathon of meetings during our two-day tour and our follow-up phone calls. That was covered in the last chapter. To be honest, we had no choice. Knowing everything about the Portland market and the submarket of the River District was the only way for me to make realistic projections about future profitability. It was the only way I could feel comfortable about making an investment. Knowing the market inside and out was the key to knowing if the project would be viable.

Fact finding is the opposite of relying on gut feelings. In the last chapter as I discussed my research method, I touched on a few important concepts that are worth defining further. These concepts are critical to understanding the total picture of the market and submarket.

Supply and Demand

When it comes to investing in property of any kind, particularly rental property, I make sure my first objective is to get an accurate read on the supply and demand in the area. I'm not talking anything complicated, just basic economics. Supply is defined as the number of rental properties available in a market or submarket.

Ideally, supply should be low and demand should be high.

Demand is defined as the number of people looking to rent. Supply is easy to determine. In Portland, we asked our emerging team, specifically brokers and property managers. They had detailed data, including property names, sizes, addresses, and dates of construction. Seek out this help; why do all this work on your own?

Demand on the other hand is a bit trickier. I estimate demand based on occupancy rates in the area. If a submarket has high occupancy, demand is great. If occupancy is low, demand is soft. Another indicator of demand is the prevalence of move-in incentives and specials. If there are a lot of move-in specials advertised, demand is low. If rental properties are offering no incentives at all, demand is high. These are some outward signs.

Another factor to consider when determining supply and demand is future supply. By future supply I mean any and all new rental property that is in various stages of development, from plan-

ning to permitting to construction. Future supply is a critical indicator of how properties in the area will perform long term.

If through your research you find that supply is greater than demand, you may want to stay away or at least keep looking for a better market. Your job of finding residents, generating cash flow, and
increasing the profitability of the property will be more difficult.
And remember, the value of a rental property increases based on its
operations and cash flow.

In Portland, demand in the River District submarket we chose
for our waterfront project certainly exceeded the existing supply.
We knew that based on our face-to-face meetings and the fact that
nothing was available in the area to rent. But by contrast, in the
small mountain community of Fountain Hills, Arizona, the opposite
is true. Here rental properties, including large apartment communities, and uncountable numbers of duplexes, condos, and single-
family homes seem to be everywhere. Many were purchased by
hopeful investors. And now they are competing head-on for a relatively small number of renters. The reasons for this lopsided market
state are no mystery. Rather they are totally explainable. Have you
figured them out yet?

The Three Drivers of Supply and Demand

Simply, there are three drivers of a market's or submarket's economics that come into play. As an investor in real estate, you'll want
to keep each of these variables in the forefront at all times. They are
true indicators of supply and demand.

EMPLOYMENT

This is the first and possibly most important indicator of demand and for good reason. If a market or submarket has lots of jobs, people will come to fill those jobs. Very basic stuff. It is a fact that jobs drive residency, so with all things being equal, property that is near to employment is in greater demand. That's not to say that people won't drive to live in a highly desirable city or town or that people won't drive to their job. But just be aware of the market condition.

When you're looking for indicators of supply and demand, look at employment. In the case of Fountain Hills, Arizona, there is little to no employment base at all. Nearly everyone who lives in the town, who is of working age, works elsewhere, like in neighboring Scottsdale. Scottsdale, by contrast, has many employers. Both Fountain Hills and Scottsdale are desirable places to live and both communities are beautiful places with excellent qualities of life. But Scottsdale wins in terms of employment and therefore in terms of demand.

People have to really want to live in Fountain Hills, and many do. But the lack of a large employer or large office complex that brings workers to the town means that Fountain Hills will find it difficult to balance the supply and demand for rental properties for many years to come. This same theory is also true for the town's retail businesses and restaurants. Employment opportunities bring customers.

It is a fact that population
follows employment.

The saying that people go where the jobs are is true. It's what attracted people to Houston, Texas, in the late 1970s and early 1980s and it's what has been attracting people to Phoenix, Arizona, for the last twenty years or so. Create jobs and people will come.

High employment can be beneficial for rental property investments, but be sure to look at the whole picture. Even communities with lots of jobs can still be overbuilt, thus throwing off the delicate balance of supply and demand. Scottsdale has been smart to limit the supply of rental properties. That has helped keep the vacancies low and the rents high. Fountain Hills, with its plentiful land by contrast, allowed the construction of too many rental units and therefore vacancies are higher and rents are lower. Fountain Hills could have been a premium rental community even without a strong employment base and once was before a boom in rental properties occurred in the mid- to late 1990s. After all, the town is a tremendous draw for winter visitors and part-time residents, a good market for rental communities.

Employment stability is also something to consider. As you evaluate your market and submarket for employment, look at how stable the employment base is. Are the companies reputable? Are their products or services in ever growing demand? Is the mix of companies diversified? These are indicators of stability. Just look at Houston in the 1980s. Rental properties were booming and then the oil industry came crashing down, taking with it banks, hotels, homebuilding companies, and numerous other businesses. Apartments were vacant all over town, so to lure renters, owners and property managers were offering ridiculous move-in packages, including six months' free rent, free televisions, and no security deposits. A significant drop in the local employment had a significant impact on the economy.

POPULATION

In a world of choices, choose to have your first—well let's face it, *all* your investment rental property where the people are! We've already established that you need a stable and growing employment base, so it makes sense that you'd also want to be in an area where there are lots of people. People who are your future customers. That may be a bit cut-and-dried for the new investor who's thinking about taking advantage of a "great deal" on a single-family home on the outskirts of town, off the beaten path. While it may be a wonderful property, and seem like a great deal, that's meaningless if nobody is around to lease it. In this book, you'll find that once the market is selected, the key to success is in the property itself and valuation is a function of its operations—how well it operates now and how well it will operate in the future. By operations, I mean how much income the property generates, what the expenses are, and what the overall profitability is. Operations success in this business relies on a market of renters.

People certainly go where the jobs are. But they also migrate to places that have a certain persona or living experience built into the area. That's a somewhat vague concept, I know, so it may be best to use examples rather than try to explain it. If you've ever been to Venice Beach in California, you know that it's a submarket of the Los Angeles market that has a definite persona or living experience. First of all, it's a California beach town that conjures up all the fun and freedom that the California Office of Tourism, Hollywood, and the Beach Boys spent decades promoting through commercials, movies, and songs. Next, it's a submarket even among other beach town markets that has a reputation for being edgy, avant-garde, and youthful.

Purchase investment property in Venice Beach and you wouldn't have to say much more. Lots of people are drawn to this lifestyle and the persona of what living in Venice Beach means. Contrast that with the Phoenix submarket of Dobson Ranch. There are rental properties in this master planned community, but the area has no real persona that drives the multitudes to it. Sure it's a nice place to live and a great place for families, but there is no major image that draws population. I'm sure most everyone reading this book has never even heard of it.

Other areas that come to mind when I think of living experience and persona are Key West, Florida, and Coronado Island, California. They both are exclusive beach resort communities. Whistler, British Columbia, is another example and the name is almost synonymous with skiing and stunning alpine scenery. Gig Harbor, Washington, is a mecca for boating enthusiasts. Aspen, Colorado, is the place to ski and be seen. And finally Scottsdale, Arizona, is known for sun, golf, spas, and shopping. These are famous places that possess personas, but there are other less famous areas in every community that have unique personas and living experiences that are known to those who live in the region.

Take some lesser known areas in Arizona: Litchfield Park, which was once known as the location of Luke Air Force Base and a lot of farms, is now readily known in the Phoenix metro area as a boomtown with lots of development, a sports arena complex in neighboring Glendale, and retail everywhere you turn. Mill Avenue, a submarket of Tempe, Arizona, is well known as a youthful, happening, artistic college center. Do you understand through these examples the concept of persona and living experience?

*Places that have clearly defined
personas are population
draws almost as powerful
as employment.*

The lure of charming buildings in towns that lack employment and a solid persona have tempted even the best of us, me included. But don't be caught! Charming buildings in towns with lots of people stay charming after the sale. And they get even more charming when they are making money. Unless you're a Vegas gambler who always tries to beat the odds, stay away from markets and submarkets that are not drawing people.

Now that you know some of the reasons why markets attract people, you'll need to know how to quantify the population in your area. Here's another time when the team comes into play. Talk to your city or town officials, visit their Web sites and set up meetings. Remember, as a taxpayer, you are paying their salaries. You are their customer. Do whatever it takes to get realistic population projections, and when they rattle off blue-sky numbers ask them to elaborate on the factors they see that are contributing to this optimistic growth scenario.

If any of your sources project population to decline, that's a bad sign. But at least they are honest. I always look for real indicators from people, not blue-sky, and value them for telling it like it is. In addition to employment and town persona as population draws, your contacts may also refer to the following:

• New highways or highway extensions. These create new traffic patterns and transform areas that once seemed a long distance away, into places that suddenly seem close by. If a new highway project is slated near that single-family home off the beaten path we talked about earlier, it may not be such a bad investment opportunity after all.

• Master planned communities. These large residential projects combine home and work and with them draw lots of people. New communities in particular are usually backed by big-dollar advertising campaigns and the older ones like Dobson Ranch mentioned earlier in this chapter become yesterday's news.

• New sports stadiums and arenas. So often the hub of urban redevelopment is a sports stadium or arena complex. These facilities bring tens of thousands of people to an area and open up all kinds of opportunities for investment real estate. The new Phoenix Coyotes hockey arena in Glendale has been one of the most important projects in the recent emergence of neighboring Litchfield Park, the boomtown we talked about earlier.

• Universities and university expansion. Universities are always population drivers because just by the nature of what they do, they bring a steady stream of students, faculty, and supporting businesses to an area. The Mill Avenue submarket of Tempe that we spoke of earlier is in walking distance of Arizona State University.

• Redevelopment areas. Our River District project in Portland is an excellent example of a redevelopment area. The ideal central locations, community goodwill, and an aura of "coolness" often associated with redevelopment makes these kinds of projects population magnets. People love the wow factor associated with before-and-after stories.

• Casinos. Casinos bring with them the masses who every weekend and a lot of weeknights want to try their luck and win big bucks. They say that in the Gold Rush of 1849 the people who made money were the ones who housed the miners and sold them goods. The same is true here, except the gamblers at the slots are the modern-day miners.

• Military bases. Not all military personnel live on the base. The property around government installations is often a good invest- ment. Just be careful of base closings, which are often in the news around government budget time.

• Regional airports. Scottsdale airport is a prime example of how valuable real estate can be around airports. The Scottsdale Airpark is a haven for small businesses and a real driver of rental communities and single-family homes in the area. A brand-new highway linking the airport to the rest of the Phoenix metro area didn't hurt either.

• Company relocations. When Boeing moved from Seattle to Chicago with it went thousands of jobs. Bad for Seattle, great for Chicago. Corporate relocations are instant population boosters.

• Major events. The 1962 World's Fair redeveloped downtown Seattle and the legacy of that event, of course, is the Space Needle, which is still a tourist attraction over forty years later. Olympic Games also have a way of transforming communities, as the 1996 games did in Atlanta and the 2000 games did in Salt Lake City. Even annual events like the Super Bowl can completely revitalize an area through huge injections of new money.

These are just a few population drivers and when you see, hear, or read about them, they are good indicators for growth.

Projects and developments such as these tend to reshape the face of a community, and change of this type is potentially lucrative for real estate investors. But there are also a few things to watch out for:

• Resilience. Make sure that the growth of a market or submarket isn't too heavily reliant on one thing. In other words, if one major employer is responsible for nearly all the population in a given area, think twice about investing. If the employer moves, so will your market. You want a market that can withstand the ups and downs. Motorola has significantly scaled back its Phoenix operations, which could have been devastating to many cities. But Phoenix's strong, diversified economy and vigorous small-business community minimized the sting.

• Economic Diversity. I steer clear of areas that don't have a good diverse economy. It's happened before and it will happen again that an entire market falls victim to an industry sector that goes bust. It happened in Pittsburgh, Houston, it happened in Detroit, and most recently in the San Francisco Bay Area when the dot-com bubble burst.

• Pioneering. Pioneers have a romantic place in history, but I make a point of never being one. Being too far out on the forefront of things can be expensive and dangerous. I try not to create the wave, simply catch a wave I see beginning to build and ride it in.

• Affordability. I always look at the affordability of housing in a particular market. If a single-family home is out of reach for most people, apartment living becomes a valuable option. This is the case in big cities like New York and San Francisco, which attract large populations, most of whom cannot afford homes. Look for markets where the cost of home ownership far exceeds the cost of renting. The closer the two variables are to each other, the harder it is to find renters and the harder it is to keep them.

LOCATION

Location is the most important thing when it comes to real estate, at least that's what everyone says. And I agree. But to me, locations have to be evaluated not based on geography alone, but based on how they measure up in relation to supply and demand. After a location has met the criterion of being in an area with good employment prospects and a growing population, I look for a few important physical features that experience has shown to be valuable:

• Great locations have drive-by visibility. The more cars that pass by your property and see your "For Rent" sign, the better your chances of success. Drive-bys are one of the most effective forms of advertising and certainly one of the most cost-efficient. When your property is on a street with no traffic, you'll have to resort to more expensive and less effective methods of advertising. This almost inevitably reduces your profitability because lower occupancy means lower cash flow.

• Great locations possess a rare quality. There's a one-of-a-kind quality about great locations that you can't find everywhere. Our Portland project was one of the only waterfront properties left in a wildly popular area. It was an island waiting to be found. That's the rare quality I'm talking about.

• Great locations are in demand. Some investors think they can't afford to even look at property in the hot locations. I hear this often at Rich Dad Seminars. But the truth is affordability is everywhere, even in the hottest neighborhoods, if you buy the property based on operational performance and not on the sale price. You'll be reading more about this concept in chapters to come, but for now know that you should never rule out A-plus neighborhoods.

Take another look at these three characteristics of great locations and what you find is that they add up to one simple truth: Great locations are low in supply and high in demand. This is at the heart of your market evaluation. Be realistic with your analysis and look at the future of the market with a keen eye on the present. Property investing should pay off now *and* later. The first step in buying right is knowing your market better than anyone else.

Focusing Your Market

After all the evaluation is said and done, you should be armed with the information you need to narrow your market. A few chapters ago we talked about goal setting. I put forth as an example the goal of finding an eight-unit property in Phoenix. The goal was as follows:

> We will acquire one eight-unit property in the Phoenix metro area within the next twelve months that will generate at least $4,000 of average annual income over the next five years.

After reading this chapter, you should now be thinking that "the Phoenix metro area" as a market is way too broad. That should be narrowed considerably. As you learn more about your own market, you will find yourself continually refining your goal and your search. That's perfectly fine. This gradual focusing is necessary and those who can't do it effectively find this type of work . . . well, a lot of work.

So let's now refine our market to Scottsdale. That's much better. And we'll focus it even further to the Old Town area, a sub-market of Scottsdale. I now know that my property choices will be in the hundreds, not the tens of thousands. Do you see what I mean about a lot of work? Focusing your market makes things manageable.

CHAPTER 5 ACTION STEPS

- Select one market in your state, preferably one close to home, that you may be interested in.
- List every submarket or separate neighborhood.
- Define and describe the employment picture of the area.
- Define and describe the unique persona of the submarket.
- Determine supply-and-demand estimates:

  ○ ask your team
  ○ read the visual signals

- Check your findings against the information in this chapter.

- Rate the submarkets based on the criteria.

- Select your submarket.

Chapter 6

Finding Your Diamond in the Rough

Identifying investment property is like dating. You want to make sure you choose wisely because you will be committing time, energy, and money. You'll be putting your heart into the effort and have big dreams of where things may lead—maybe a long-term commitment, maybe marriage. Dating just anyone, like targeting any old property, can be a huge time waster and even cost you a lot of money. I speak from experience on both counts.

After the last five chapters you can see that choosing wisely involves setting a goal, building your team, and evaluating and focusing on your market. There's a lot of preparation required before you actually select a property. And what you are looking for isn't necessarily the winner of the beauty pageant, but a diamond in the rough. This is the one with the most potential, and potential as you'll see in later chapters means bottom-line dollars.

Time and again, investors start at this stage—they work on finding a property and completely skip the preparation work. This is
why the word "risk" is so often associated with real estate. Selecting
the property should come only after you have assembled a team to
assist you, decided upon your goal, and done the work of identifying a market or submarket. Never should it come before. It requires
a level of trust, but like I always say:

Trust but verify.

By now you have found your market and a submarket or submarkets within it. The next step is finding the property that will
achieve your income and profitability goals within your chosen area.
This chapter will show you how. To do that, I'll take you through the
same steps I use to find property. We'll save the evaluation of that
property for Chapter 7.

This chapter and the one that follows are critical to your success in this business because this book isn't about just buying
property, it's about buying property right. For the right price, in the
right area, with the right expectation to achieve your goal. This is
the only way I buy, and the reason is simple. When you buy right
you spend your days tending a garden rather than digging out rocks.
Life is too short.

Setting Target Property Parameters

Let's go back to the hypothetical goal of finding an eight-unit property. In the last chapter we focused our market to the Old Town

area of Scottsdale. Now it's time to focus our property parameters. Our goal currently reads:

> We will acquire one eight-unit property in Old Town Scottsdale within the next twelve months that will generate at least $4,000 of average annual income over the next five years.

You know what's coming, don't you? We need to get more specific about our eight-unit property. That's a vague term. When I was just starting out in this business, I searched for property myself. Now I hire someone to sift through property that is listed and not listed to find what fits my parameters. You might think that's a luxury only established investors can afford. Not so. The person who works for me is a broker and he gets paid when he finds a deal that closes. Anyone can afford this kind of help. And helpful it was for both of us. Together we were able to focus our search, hold each other accountable, and improve our chances of success. Now, we meet for an hour every week. It's not a huge commitment of time, but it adds a lot of value.

For me, it helps a lot to have a precise idea of the kind of property I'm interested in. It saves a lot of time, keeps my broker and me focused, and helps make the work manageable. I am very specific about what I want to consider. For example, we're looking in one market right now for a 150-plus-unit community in a good location with high visibility, drive-by traffic on major streets, and constructed after 1988. Even more specifically, I'm looking for owner-managed properties where the owners live out of state and have just one or two properties in the entire city.

These parameters are not arbitrary. I want properties that are of

substantial size so we can afford to have a professional property manager on site to handle the day-to-day issues. That works well within
my company's structure. The year 1988 is important because many
properties older than that take a lot of money to bring up to the standard of other apartment buildings in the area. You will find it's normal to replace roofs, paint, install new carpeting, and so forth. But if
all the other apartment buildings in the area have washer-dryer
hookups and yours doesn't, you will either have to spend lots of
money remodeling and updating if possible, or charge below-market
rents. Neither is a good alternative. See what I mean about knowing
your market?

By targeting properties that have owner-managers who live out
of state, I have found there is a higher likelihood that they are not
managing the property to its full potential. There are a number of
likely reasons for this:

• Travel. Often people buy property in hot markets that are
far away from their own hometowns and underestimate how
much time and energy is required to manage it. Add in travel time
and expenses to that, and you can see why absentee ownership is
prevalent.

• Complacency. It's easy for out-of-towners to lose interest and
become complacent over time. Especially if they are making money
and their property isn't one they drive by every day.

• Perception. Many owners wrongly believe that the investment real estate business is an investment and not a business. They
think it is like a stock or a bond that they can buy and forget. In truth
it is a business they need to operate.

- Lack of information. This actually happened with a property my company manages; the owners have no idea at all about the market, the market potential, or the condition of the property itself. The owner bought it sight unseen! That is beyond my comprehension.

Learning about your market to the level of detail that will make you successful in this business continues during this phase of the process. At last, you are drilling down to individual properties and there are a lot out there. You'll want to make sure your target market isn't too big or you will end up considering thousands of properties. Recall in the last chapter the concept of markets and submarkets. In San Diego, you have the Gaslamp Quarter, Balboa Park, Sea World Area, Old Town, and Coronado Island. In New York, you have Greenwich Village, SoHo, Upper West Side, Upper East Side, TriBeCa, Harlem, Midtown. Then there are submarkets within those areas. Know where you want to be specifically, and start there. You may have to work your way outward or to other submarkets if there is nothing in your first-choice market.

The more established you become in this business and the more people you tell about your goal, the more opportunities will come your way. At least they will appear as opportunities; many of them are distractions cloaked as opportunities. As tempted as you will be to jump on a plane and fly from California to Florida or from Virginia to Texas when you see what looks or sounds like a great deal, stay focused and resolute on your goal. It's too overwhelming to try to consider everything at once.

Becoming an Expert

You need to become an expert in the submarket you select and a good deal of that learning happens during the market evaluation phase. But it also happens as you are evaluating properties. Adopt the mind-set that learning is ongoing and forever. You never know enough about a market and the market is constantly changing. I look at everything around me in terms of real estate. Call it a sickness, but every story I read in the paper, every conversation I have, every retail center I see, every stoplight erected on a street corner, every new employer or employer expansion has real estate implications to me. I see them everywhere. My eye is trained. But if your senses are not as honed as mine, here are some guidelines to help to achieve expert status:

USE YOUR RESEARCH

The research you have done in preparation for property investment should be organized and usable. I have market and property information organized so that I can refer to it at any time. Just because I'm in the property-targeting stage doesn't mean that I stop looking at my research. The work that you did before should become your bible. Scan it more intensely now that you've chosen your market more specifically.

The research that you did months ago should be continually updated. Real estate is a fast-moving business, so I do research all the time. Anything that I see that pertains to my target markets I catalogue and keep. Anything that pertains to markets I'm not currently targeting I catalogue and track. You just never know when a sleepy community like Litchfield Park, Arizona, will pop onto the radar and become a boomtown, unless you track it! Then, you'll see it coming often before anyone else.

READ EVERYTHING

I read every newspaper I can get my hands on in our target markets. Sure I glance at the property listings, but more important, I look at the news, the sports, the neighborhood happenings. That's where I get a real picture of the market. For example, I look for any big events that relate to the area. Take, for instance, the school district passing a bond initiative to build another elementary school. That's the kind of news that will draw people to a community. Similarly, things like new retail centers, rezoning of a land parcel, declarations of historic landmarks, crime reports, all have real estate implications. So do feature stories that rank communities with the wealthiest zip codes, that have the lowest crime, and that have the best school test scores. Even the morning traffic reports tell you something about a market and its desirability.

LOOK AROUND

Before you seriously target a property, look hard at the neighborhood. I know this from experience. There are several apartment buildings we manage but do not own. One building, when we took over managing it, was so full of gang members, drugs, and violence that anyone reputable was long gone. It was a haven for criminals. Worst of all, it was right in the center of a neighborhood riddled with crime. Things were so bad that in one apartment I entered during the site visit there was an M-16 propped up next to the door.

Honest truth. We managed to clean up the apartment community through mass evictions and the hiring of off-duty city police officers to patrol the property twenty-four hours a day. We made it undesirable for criminals and slowly good people moved back in. But the apartment building was all we cleaned up. We did not change the neighborhood. And that's the lesson. You cannot change the neighborhood, so make sure the property is in a place that you're prepared to manage. As a reminder, you want to be riding the front of the wave, not creating the wave. There's a difference. Let the hero be Spiderman.

LISTEN MORE THAN YOU TALK

Listen for the word on the street. The buzz. Not just what the news is saying, but rather what people are informally talking about. Shop owners, other apartment owners, neighbors, utility meter readers, cable technicians, mail carriers, UPS carriers, everyone who spends time in the market. Listen to what the insiders on your team are talking about. Listen to where they say they are going next. But don't be fooled by rumors. If you hear something, verify it with your team of experts and others with opinions that matter. I believe in my network, and I make a point of keeping in touch with everyone in it regularly. There are people who I go to lunch with just to listen to what they have to say and to find out what they are doing. Eventually, you'll hear about things you'll read in the papers weeks later. That's being on the front of the wave.

JOIN A BUSINESS NETWORKING GROUP OR TRADE ASSOCIATION

Often you can find groups that meet regularly that have similar goals as you. I am active in the local Arizona Multihousing Association as well as in the National Apartment Association and the Institute of Real Estate Management. These are good places to meet people who might be valuable additions to my team, to find people I may want to hire, and to stay on top of issues that could affect my investments.

Search on Your Own or Hire Out?

You can do all this pavement pounding yourself and it's probably a good idea regardless of which path you choose—to hire or not to hire. For one, you'll be smarter about the property you inevitably purchase, and two, it will make you a better judge of properties presented to you by the broker you hire. But hiring this service out has its benefits.

Brokers will help you find property in your market and will do it on a 100 percent commission basis. That's what they do. When you close the sale, a commission is paid, often by the seller. First, brokers tend to specialize in their markets, so choose one who is a specialist in your target market. If you make a good selection your broker can be a wealth of information to you. They know the new retail stores that are coming into town, the new roads and highway projects, even employers who are expanding or downsizing. Second, brokers save you a lot of time. They will be able to find property quickly and present you with choices. Third, brokers can make calls to property owners for you so you can cover more ground. You probably won't strike a deal on the first call or even the tenth call. Finally—and this is a big benefit—there are no up-front costs to you.

If you choose to hire a broker, make sure you have a person you trust and that he or she matches your high degree of integrity. As with everything, there are good brokers and bad brokers. A good broker will be focused on building a relationship with you long term versus working to obtain a commission. Good brokers really do know what's going on in the market. Moreover, they are *known* for knowing what's going on in the market. They are quoted in the paper. They are active in the community. Good brokers communicate with you often via letters and e-mail. They are proactive in the way they do business with you by following up on the details. They are usually the top producers in the market. Remember, trust but verify.

*The hardest road is the one you travel
alone. No man is an island.*

Nothing Is for Sale

After weeks of narrowing your market, defining your submarket, learning everything there is to know, and talking with business leaders in the community, your broker gives you the bad news: There's nothing for sale that meets your criteria. So now what do you do? Should you move on? Start looking in another part of town? Wait until something suitable comes on the market? Of course not. You simply make a move to buy a property that isn't technically for sale!

I believe when a property is listed, it's too late. By that point, you're competing with other prospective buyers, and working with a seller who has established a purchase price that he or she may want to stick to. When I see a wave worth riding in a particular area, I don't wait for the "For Sale" sign to get plunked into the ground. I go for it. Often, the "For Sale" sign never makes it in the ground because other people recognized the trend before you did and beat you to it.

The issue here is about the real estate and buying it right. It's not about whether the property is for sale or not. You've heard the saying "everything is for sale, for the right price." Well, the same is true here. Most of the properties we purchased in 2002 were not listed for sale. They were all acquired by making the first move and contacting the owner. So how do you do that?

Contacting the Owner

When you begin working in the investment real estate industry, you'll quickly realize there is no privacy in this world. I mean it. In less than ten minutes on the Internet, I can find the value of the house you are living in, how many square feet, how many bedrooms and baths, what you paid for it and when, what it looks like, where it is located, and in many cases see an actual aerial photograph of it taken by a satellite camera! Does that surprise you? Well you won't be surprised for long because this is exactly the type of information you'll be pulling off the Internet yourself as you investigate properties.

Everything I mentioned in the paragraph above is a matter of public record. None of the sources to find this information are illegal or shady. In fact most all of them are government agencies. My point here is simply, if I can find out that information about your house, you can find it out about any building you are interested in purchasing. That includes the name, address, and phone number of the owner.

That's one easy way to find out information about a property, and you're always better off knowing as much as you can. You can also take the direct approach and ask residents, the property manager, real estate brokers who work the area, the tax assessor's office, and title companies.

Sometimes as you look for the owners of a property you'll discover it is owned by a corporation, not a person. Don't let that stop you. Call the corporation commission in your state and you'll be able to get the names, addresses, and phone numbers of the corporation officers. Nothing is secret!

Once you have enough facts about a property, you'll want to call the owner. This is the best way to find out more about a property and see if the owner would entertain an offer. Making the phone call can be scary at first but not if you are honest from the get-go. There's no need to tap-dance. Just ask the question and be prepared for rejection.

To help you through the first conversation with the property owner, I've set up the following table. It maps out a typical conversation and what to say.

The Owner Says	You Say	Comments
Hello.	Hello, my name is (your name). Are you the owner of the property at (state the address)?	At this point the owner is thinking you are a mortgage broker trying to get him to refinance. He'll want to hang up.
Yes I am.	Your property is one of ten on the list that fits my parameters of an eight-plex in Old Town Scottsdale and I'd like to talk to you about buying it.	Now the owner is thinking, "Who is this guy and is he reputable? Is he a broker just trying to get a sales listing or is this a real buyer?"
I might be interested in that. What did you have in mind?	First thing is I'm not a broker looking for a listing, and I'd like to say that everything we talk about here is confidential and I am prepared to send you a confidentiality agreement. I'll fax it to you immediately, signed by me.	The owner is thinking the confidentiality agreement is very professional. He likes that. This sounds legitimate.

(Table continued)

The Owner Says	*You Say*	*Comments*
What kind of money are we talking about?	I'm not prepared to make an offer today, but once I find out more about your property and its operations, I'll get a formal offer to you within a week. If you can give me some basic information, I could get an offer started right away. My offer will be based on a return on my investment. And I won't know what that return is until I look at the operations of the property.	At this point, you are not in a position to make any kind of offer because you don't know how the property is operating. Remember, buying right is about buying based on operating performance. The seller may be reluctant to give this information or he or she may be open to it. You must make the owner understand that he or she is risking nothing by giving you this information and that he won't ever get an offer unless he does.
What kind of information do you need?	For starters, I'll need the rent roll [which is a listing of the units and how much they rent for] and your current occupancy. I'll also need your operating expenses.	The rent roll and current occupancy rate are the two key indicators of how a property is operating. These two pieces of information are critical to establishing the purchase price as you'll see in the next chapter. You will likely find you are educating the seller here and helping him determine what the property is really worth.

The Owner Says	*You Say*	*Comments*
I don't want to send you that information.	Okay, I can make you an offer without this information, but unless I know how the property is operating, the offer may change dramatically should we decide to go forward and I *will* see this information during the buying process. I'd rather be informed now and provide you a reasonable offer right up front. If nothing else, you'll get an assessment of how much your property is worth. I'd rather not have to renegotiate further down the line.	The owner needs to understand that there is no risk here. This is information you'll need to know sooner or later, and sooner is better. As you'll see in the next chapter, you'll review the property operations in detail before you buy anything, so there's no point keeping this information secret.
Tell me a little bit about you and your company.	We are a real estate investment company in (your town) and are looking for properties in this one-mile area near the Old Town Scottsdale center. With the right information we are prepared to make an offer within one week.	If the owner asks this question, be prepared with your thirty-second speech about your company. The owner at this point may want to have one more credibility check. The idea here is to make sure he or she knows you are professional and credible and that you mean business. You must demonstrate that you are capable of pulling off the deal and that you are decisive about what you want.

(Table continued)

The Owner Says	*You Say*	*Comments*
That sounds fine. I'll get you the information you need.	To summarize then: You're going to get me the rent roll and the occupancy and operating expenses by tomorrow morning. I'm going to send you my confidentiality agreement immediately, and I'm going to send you my offer letter within a week of receiving your information.	To conclude the call, restate the action items and set up the deliverable dates.
I'll look forward to hearing from you. Thank you. Goodbye.	Great. I'll get back to you. Thank you for your time. Goodbye.	Conclude the call on a cordial, optimistic note.

If the Seller Is Not Interested

The Owner Says	*You Say*	*Comments*
No, I'm not interested.	I see. Can I send you my information and keep in touch? And please call me if you reconsider.	In the event of rejection, don't burn the bridge. Many of the properties I own today were originally owned by people who were not interested in selling at first. Stay in contact with these people and call once a quarter. Put them on your mailing list.

Contacting the owner can be easy, provided you steer the conversation in the direction just demonstrated. The goal with the first phone call is to try to educate the seller and build a relationship. There are two kinds of sellers: one trusting and the other untrusting. Some people may give you lots of information and that helps. Others may be secretive and not want to divulge anything. Either way, keep accurate notes of everything stated, because what is stated in this conversation is highly material to any future negotiations.

Learning and Networking

Whether your first contact with a property owner leads to an eventual purchase or not is not that important. The whole exercise is worth the practice and the learning that can only come from doing. I find that no matter how much I think I know about a market, I always come away from conversations with property owners knowing more than I did before. You'll be surprised at how quickly you will come to know a market or submarket by talking to property owners within it.

As a side benefit I also know I've established another entire network of people for future leads. I've found several properties this way. One building I now own came my way from a property owner who didn't want to sell the building I initially contacted him about. Instead, we ended up doing a deal on another property a few miles away. This happens often.

This whole process is about becoming an expert, putting out feelers, and getting some action going, so don't be discouraged if your first calls are rejections. It's like fishing. You put the worm on the hook, cast it out, and see what comes back. Eventually one or two will bite and then the real action begins. And that's the focus of our next chapter, determining the initial valuation of the property.

CHAPTER 6 ACTION STEPS

- Narrow your target property parameters further based on your initial review of properties in your targeted submarket.

- Find out everything you can about the properties in your targeted submarket:

  ○ use your team to help you get specifics on every property
  ○ create a spreadsheet or chart that compares, at a glance, the rents, features, and amenities

- Continue to read the business, government, and news sections of newspapers and recognize how any changes can impact real estate.

- Find all the real estate associations in your area and join them. Attend their functions and make a point of meeting people.

- Decide whether you want a broker to help you find property.

- Locate and target a few properties you may be interested in buying.

- Find the owner information on the Internet.

- Call and meet with residents, shop owners, and property managers to get more information.

- Get ready to make your first phone calls (you'll need the information in Chapter 7 to follow up on any properties that may be for sale, so hold off on making your calls!).

Is It Really a Diamond?

Someone once told me that the average person remembers only three to five concepts in a business book. Just three to five! I know already in this book there have been dozens of concepts presented. So which ones are going to be remembered and which ones forgotten? I found this statement hard to believe until I started to think back on the books that I read recently. And I had to admit that if I remembered three concepts in each of them I was lucky. (I always knew I was average.)

Well, I'm not going to assume that with this book I'm going to change the reading comprehension rate of the typical human. And I'm not going to take it personally if after reading this book, you don't retain every single thing. But I will be disappointed if you don't remember the concepts in this chapter. In fact, if you forget everything else you read in this book, this is the one chapter I hope you not only remember, but refer to often. Because if you master the process I'm revealing in the pages ahead, your life as an investor in rental property will be infinitely easier. Infinitely!

It's true that your success in this business is the result of your preparation. That's the message and the purpose of the early chapters of this book. But regardless of how prepared you are, you can create a disaster for yourself in a matter of seconds if you can't tell a diamond from a cubic zirconium. That's the time it takes to sign your name on the dotted line of a bad deal.

I know that sounds pretty scary. There is little gray area separating a good deal from a bad one; and to me, gray area is made up of black and white. A deal is either good or bad and fortunately a bad one is easy to define. It is simply a deal where the numbers don't work. In other words it's when the projected cash flow—income minus total expenses—equals a low or negative number.

In good deals the numbers work.
In bad deals, they don't.

Does this seem terribly obvious? Of course it does. But you'd be surprised how many times investors ignore this simple truth. They purchase property based on the seller's asking price, or something close to it, instead of the operational performance of the property. Here are a few principles about property investing we need to get out on the table right now:

- The seller's asking price is irrelevant.
- You determine the property value, which becomes your offer.

- With multiple units, the property value is based on the current cash flow of the property.

These three principles are the foundation for everything else in this chapter. That's because in this chapter, I will walk you through my own personal system for determining property valuations for multiple units. It's called the Five Step Property Evaluation and I've used it for the past fifteen years with outstanding results. Here it is in a nutshell:

1. Verify property income.
2. Verify expenses.
3. Determine net operating income.
4. Find the capitalization rate and valuation.
5. Calculate the loan payment and your profit or cash on cash.

I use those five steps to come up with the initial cash flow for the property and arrive at an offer price. To do that, we look at everything associated with expenses—including our loan payments—and everything associated with income during our analysis. In the end we have a solid picture of the bottom line for the property and are in a position to make our offer.

You'll realize the importance of this process when you think of it this way. Would you put your money into a mutual fund without looking at its past earnings performance? Would you put your money in an annuity if you didn't know the annual interest rate? Probably not. Well, why invest in real estate without a reasonable estimate of what your return on investment will be? In real estate investing, return on investment is also called "cash on cash," and it is your net cash flow as a percentage of your down payment.

For instance, if you put $100,000 down on a property and it brings in $1,000 of income per month, your cash on cash is 12 percent per year. Not bad. But if that same property brought in $500 per month, your 6 percent return may not seem worth your time. As you read on, you'll see why it's too early to make that judgment.

Furthermore, the process I will describe in this chapter will enable you to value property without actually doing a physical inspection. You heard me correctly. In over 95 percent of the offers we make, I do not visit the community before I complete the valuation and make an offer. What could I really gain by doing a property visit that I couldn't learn from the seller at this point? If I personally visited every single property my company is considering, we would be forever visiting properties and have no time left to actually purchase them. At this stage, I rely on my team to fill in any gaps I may have in my knowledge about a property.

Case in point, we just opened escrow last week on a 172-unit apartment building in Glendale, Arizona. I had one of my team members visit the property while we reviewed the numbers. The negotiation lasted about three weeks as we went back and forth on the offer price. The figures we used for our evaluation came entirely from the seller and the broker listing the property. Don't misunderstand. I will not buy the property without walking each and every unit, performing a thorough inspection, and verifying the numbers. I just let my team do a lot of the preliminary screening for me.

Another property in the works right now is in San Diego. We're in the second round of negotiations and I have yet to actually visit the property. This shows the level of confidence I have in my partners and my team members. They feel good about the property, so

I feel good about the property; I trust them implicitly on what could be a $66 million acquisition.

My point with these two stories is that offers are nothing more than an opportunity to look at the numbers and make an educated guess about how a property will perform in terms of cash flow, based on a brief, top-line evaluation. As you'll see in a later chapter, you'll find out about the property in minute detail once you "tie up" the property by getting it under contract. That's when you begin the inspection period known as due diligence. But let's not get ahead of ourselves. Let's take a look at the Five-Step Property Valuation. That will give us the information that we need to say "go" or "no go" to a property investment.

Step 1: Verify Property Income

Even if the seller discloses the current income on a rental property either through a pro forma document or verbally, verify it. Property income is the first and perhaps the most important factor when it comes to buying investment property. Unlike your primary residence mortgage, which the bank secures with your own assets, rental investment property loans are most often secured by the income-generating potential of the property itself. If you don't verify income right up front, you'll have to do it later for the bank, so there's no time like the present. And this one variable will tell you without going any further whether this property is worth any more of your time.

Before we get too far, let's define some terms. There are three types of income to consider with any property: actual income, actual potential income and future potential income.

• Actual income: The total income the property generated in the prior twelve months.

• Actual potential income: The total income the property could have generated in the prior twelve months had all units been 100 percent occupied and had the owner taken advantage of all other income opportunities.

• Future potential income: The total income the property could generate at today's market rents, 100 percent occupancy, and taking full advantage of all other income opportunities.

Traditionally, many property owners will try to sell their property based on the future potential income. It is in your best interest to buy it at the actual income. That's the way I like to buy—based on the way the property is currently running and the amount of money it is currently making. I think of that as "wholesale." If you buy property based on how it *could* run and the income it *could* generate in the future—the future potential income—I call that buying it "retail." Try to avoid retail purchases at all costs. Buying right means buying at wholesale. When you buy wholesale, your mortgage is lower and right out of the gate that means you are maximizing your profitability on the property.

With the important distinction between retail and wholesale out in the open, trust but verify all numbers listed on the back of the sales brochures you get from brokers and sellers. These sales brochures have a fairly standard format. Usually on the front there is a photo of the building and on the back are a lot of numbers that depict the property's operations performance. You simply cannot accept these numbers as fact, since they are often inflated.

Before you start a rumor that Ken McElroy is a broker hater, know that on the bottom of every sales brochure I've ever seen are these words:

> This brokerage company makes no warranty or representation about the content of this brochure. It is your responsibility to independently confirm its accuracy and competencies. Any projections, opinions, assumptions or estimates used are for example only and do not represent the current or future performance of the property.

This disclaimer makes it pretty clear that a smart investor must verify each and every number in this brochure. If you don't, they are basically saying with this one statement: It's your own fault.

Here's how you verify the income from the numbers on a typical property pro forma in a sales brochure. The information I'll use in this example is from an actual property in Phoenix, Arizona. Let's start with unit mix and rent schedule.

UNIT MIX AND RENT SCHEDULE

The unit mix and rent schedule is a table that is usually in rental property brochure pro formas. It lists the number of units, the type, square footage, and rent. Its purpose is to give you a picture of the income, by unit and overall for the property. Here's an example:

Number of Units	Type	Sq. Ft.	Total Sq. Ft.	Rent	Total Rent	Rent/ Sq. Ft.
6	1/1	650	3900	*$475	$2,850	$0.73
2	2/1	750	1500	*$575	$1,150	$0.77
8	Averages	675	5400	*$500	$4,000	$0.74

*Current rents average $480 for the two-bedroom units and $422 for the one-bedroom units.

I use unit mix and rent schedule tables to verify the rent income on properties, and from experience I have yet to ever find one in a pro forma that accurately depicted the actual income picture. That's why it's important to know how to read and analyze this information. Let's look a little closer.

Number of Units	Type	Sq. Ft.	Total Sq. Ft.	Rent	Total Rent	Rent/ Sq. Ft.
6	1/1	650	3900	*$475	$2,850	$0.73
2	2/1	750	1500	*$575	$1,150	$0.77
8	Averages	675	5400	*$500	$4,000	$0.74

*Current rents average $480 for the two-bedroom units and $422 for the one-bedroom units.

With this information, the owner is telling you that the total rent for the eight units on this property is $4,000 per month based on the rents as listed in the "Total Rent" column. But on this particular table, the seller put asterisks next to the rents to indicate that the actual rents are lower. Significantly lower—see the small print. An inexperienced buyer might look at this table and conclude that the $4,000 is the actual income of the property. But the fact is, and by the seller's own admission, which is rare by the way, this $4,000 is the future potential income based on higher rents, which may or may not be at the market rent levels.

Let's see how the income picture changes when we insert into the table the actual rents for this property.

Number of Units	Type	Sq. Ft.	Total Sq. Ft.	Rent	Total Rent	Rent/ Sq. Ft.
6	1/1	650	3900	$422	$2,532	$0.65
2	2/1	750	1500	$480	$960	$0.64
8	Averages	675	5400	$437	$3,492	$0.65

Now that the actual rent numbers are in this table, it is clear that the rents used by the seller or broker were a full $63 per unit higher than what the property is actually generating. Over a twelve-month period, that equates to $6,048. If you would have bought this property based on the seller's pro forma, your income would have been more than $6,000 below what you expected. That's not good.

But what if the seller doesn't reveal the actual rent numbers in the small print on a brochure pro forma, and they usually aren't. Then you must request a rent roll and use those numbers for your calculations. You should even verify the small print rents on a brochure such as this one by comparing them to the actual rent roll. Trust, but verify.

WHAT ABOUT VACANCIES AND OTHER INCOME?

At this point, we have verified the actual potential income for the property. Remember that's the income the property could generate at current rents with 100 percent occupancy. But certainly, it is highly unlikely that this property is or will be 100 percent occupied every day of every year from now until eternity. So we have to take into account vacancy and turnover from residents moving in and out. And while we're at it, we should consider any other income generated from sources like laundry facilities, parking, and so on.

The typical pro forma lists these values as well. And surprise! these numbers, too, I have found to be inaccurate most of the time. Vacancies are usually understated and other income is usually over-inflated. The key here is to try to project what the vacancies and other income will be in the future. It's nice to know where you've been, but where you're going is really more important. That's why the windshield is so big and the rearview mirror is so small.

Common sense will tell you that if an apartment is not rented, it is not producing income, and that reduces your cash flow. Even if the vacancy rate is listed on the pro forma, verify it with the property manager on your team. He or she will be able to tell you if the vacancy rate listed is at, above, or below the average of the market and will know this because vacancies are mostly a function of supply and demand within the market. You can also find this information by looking at the monthly rent rolls and move-in dates on the leases.

The income section on the pro forma is where the seller lists the property's income and the vacancy rate. It shows the income from rent, minus the average vacancy for the property, and adds to it the other income the property generates. The typical pro forma income table looks like the one below, which contains numbers taken directly from the property in Phoenix. In this real-world example, the seller or broker is *reporting* a total income for the property to be $45,120 per year, using a 7 percent vacancy rate and $480 in other income. That seems pretty good. But look at the rent figure. It's based on the inflated rent numbers listed on the unit mix and rent schedule. You remember those; they were the ones with the asterisks. That's not good.

Income

		Seller Pro Forma
Gross Scheduled Rent		$48,000
Less: Vacancy	7%	$(3,360)
Net Rental Income		$44,640
Plus Other Income		$480
Total Income		$45,120

Take a look below at what happens to our total income when we insert the *real* rents in the *projected* column. Keep in mind the rent value is the only thing we have changed in this analysis. The total income for the property falls by $5,669 ($45,120 − $39,451). That's a lot of money, especially if you were counting on it. Reality hurts—particularly if you don't see it coming.

Income

		Seller Pro Forma	Prior Year Actuals	Our Projected
Gross Scheduled Rent		$48,000		$41,904
Less: Vacancy	7%	$(3,360)		$(2,933)
Net Rental Income		$44,640		$38,971
Plus Other Income		$480		$480
Total Income		$45,120	$41,800	$39,451

Now, look at the three figures for total income: the seller pro forma number of $45,120; the prior year actual number of $41,800; and our projected number of $39,451. First, let's compare the seller pro forma income number with the prior year actual income number. What this tells you is that the reported seller pro forma income number is $3,320 more than the income from prior year operations ($45,120 − $41,800). The seller is implying that you can improve the operations from what it was last year, and they don't even know what kind of manager you'll be! This isn't flattery. It's more like a "fast one."

As I'm sure you have guessed, when I formulate my offer I disregard the other two income numbers and use my own projected figure, the one that takes into account the *real* property rents. The best part of this strategy is that because the numbers are real, they are easy to defend during the negotiation process.

This is how easy it is to verify income and how easy it is to catch these kinds of inconsistencies in the numbers. As I mentioned, income is often inflated, so don't be shocked if the difference between the numbers on the pro forma and the numbers you project are in the thousands. That is common.

Before we leave the topic of income, let's address future potential income. Recall that future potential income is the total income the property *could* generate at today's market rents, 100 percent occupancy, and by taking full advantage of all other income opportunities. You may find through your income verification process that the reported rents are well below the market. This could be your "Advance to Boardwalk" card, so keep it close to your vest. It's this kind of upside potential that property investors dream about. With income verified, it's now time to turn our attention to expenses.

Step 2: Verify Expenses

Expenses are the second important variable to consider. As I mentioned earlier, the definition of net operating income is income minus expenses. In the previous section, we showed you the specifics you need to review to estimate the income potential of a property. In this section, you'll see how to assess the expenses.

Just as we did when we verified income, you'll want to get a picture of the current expenses. Unlike the income calculation where our goal was to be 100 percent on the money in terms of accuracy, with expenses the goal is to get reasonably close. We'll find out all the minute details later in the game. This is another area where your team of pros can help you.

Regardless of whether you will be using a property management company or not, calling one to visit the property and help you assess everything involved in running the place is a good idea, particularly if you are looking at a multi-unit building. Just call and say, "I'm looking at buying an eight-unit building, and I'm not sure if I want to run it myself or hire a company to do it. I'd like to show you the building and talk with you about it." The hour or so you spend with the property management representative will be a good investment of time. And if you have to pay that person an hourly consulting fee, it's worth it. Make the objective of the meeting twofold. First, you'll want to learn what it will take to run the property, and second, you'll want to get insight on how to minimize expenses.

Keep in mind, at this point in the process your goal is to get an idea of the ongoing services and repairs as well as upgrades the building may need. Later in the process, you'll go into lots more detail. This is the time to put rough numbers on paper and analyze if the cost of the needed repairs will still allow you to be profitable. There is a real balancing act between spending enough to get the place in shape and overspending. Again, your property management representative can help you determine many of these costs.

The goal throughout this whole exercise is to get a picture of where your expenses are and try to find ways to do things better, smarter, and for less money. Those increase your net income and increase your profitability. So what are the expenses? To answer that question, we'll turn to the pro forma expense table. It shows the seller's anticipated expenses for the coming year (the pro forma column) and the actual expenses for the prior year. Here's what this table looks like for the property in Phoenix we're using as our real-world example:

Expenses

	Per Unit	Seller Pro Forma	Prior Year Actuals
Repairs and Maintenance	$838	$6,700	$8,010
Utilities	$409	$3,273	$3,273
Real Estate Taxes	$425	$3,400	$3,400
Insurance	$125	$1,000	$1,000
Replacement Reserve	$150	$1,200	
Total Expenses	$1,947/unit	$15,573	$15,683
	$2.88/sq. ft.		

Let's analyze these figures in much more detail and add our projected expenses. First we'll look at "Repairs and Maintenance."

	Per Unit	Seller Pro Forma	Prior Year Actuals	Our Projected
Repairs and Maintenance	$838	$6,700	$8,010	$8,010

The first thing that caught my eye on this table was a seller pro forma value lower than the prior year actuals number. For some reason this seller or broker wants buyers to believe that the repairs and maintenance will actually go down! In fact, this seller predicts repair and maintenance to go down by over $1,300 from the actual prior year costs. Here's a rule of thumb: As properties age, repair and maintenance costs go up. Common sense says expenses in the coming year will be the same or more. We'll keep it simple here. For purposes of my projections I will use the prior year actuals number of $8,010 knowing that even this number could be low. Time will tell.

Next we'll look at the utilities:

	Per Unit	Seller Pro Forma	Prior Year Actuals	Our Projected
Utilities	$409	$3,273	$3,273	$3,273

The seller's pro forma utilities figure appears to be in line with the actual expenses from the prior year, but let me caution you that utilities normally have standard rate increases from year to year. In this pro forma the seller projects no increases. For now, we'll use the seller pro forma number, but you can get a very realistic projection simply by contacting the utility companies.

How about the next line in our expense table: "Real Estate Taxes"?

	Per Unit	Seller Pro Forma	Prior Year Actuals	Our Projected
Real estate taxes	$425	$3,400	$3,400	$3,400

Real estate tax expenses are simple to determine with almost pinpoint accuracy. The data is usually available on the Internet in most areas. Simply go to the county assessor Web site and locate the property search area of the site. Then just type in the property address to get the current figures. In most cases you'll see not only the prior year property tax amounts, but also projections for one or two years out. Focus on the future and use the next year's assessment as your projection.

Understand that property sales often trigger tax increases, so you may want to consult with your real estate tax team member about this. For the purpose of the expense evaluation, I'll just say I found the seller's figures to be accurate.

Next is the insurance expense line.

	Per Unit	Seller Pro Forma	Prior Year Actuals	Our Projected
Insurance	$125	$1,000	$1,000	$1,200

Insurance is a fast-moving business and rates can vary widely from company to company. My suggestion is that you get a couple of insurance agents to bid on the property and use that number in your projections. As your business grows you can bundle all your properties under a bulk insurance program, which generates substantial savings. We do this and secure bids annually. For our expense analysis on the Phoenix property, we will increase our projected figure to $1,200 per year based on my personal experience.

Finally, we'll look at "Replacement Reserve":

	Per Unit	Seller Pro Forma	Prior Year Actuals	Our Projected
Replacement Reserve	$150	$1,200		$1,200

The replacement reserve is the funds you put aside for the inevitable replacement of capital items such as appliances, carpets, countertops, roofs, and so on. I get really nervous when I see that the seller did not spend a dime on the property in the prior year as this table indicates. Moreover, the broker or seller projected an additional $1,200 for the new buyer and trust me, this is no gift. This tells me that this property has some deferred maintenance and it's probably more than the $1,200 figure. For purposes of this offer, I will keep the number at $1,200 for now, but after I walk the property I may have a very different opinion.

ADJUSTED EXPENSES

At this point, we have the numbers we need to complete our analysis. To do this, we get out our calculator and run the expense totals. Keep in mind that we haven't visited the property and once we do, we may adjust these numbers again based on what we find during our inspections.

Here are our totals:

Expenses

	Per Unit	Seller Pro Forma	Prior Year Actuals	Our Projected
Repairs and Maintenance	$838	$6,700	$8,010	$8,010
Utilities	$409	$3,273	$3,273	$3,273
Real Estate Taxes	$425	$3,400	$3,400	$3,400
Insurance	$125	$1,000	$1,000	$1,200
Replacement Reserve	$150	$1,200		$1,200
Total Expenses	$1,947/unit $2.88/sq. ft.	$15,573	$15,683	$17,083

Take a look at the total expenses line to see how the numbers differ. As you can see, the range is significant, from $15,573 to $17,083. That's a $1,510 ($17,083 − $15,573) difference between our projected expenses to operate the property and the seller's pro forma expenses. Had you bought this property without going through this exercise, that $1,510 may have been money right off your bottom line.

Step 3: Determine Net Operating Income

After you have determined your income potential for the property and you have a good estimate of the expenses, you need to determine the net operating income (NOI). This is a very important number because you will eventually base your offer on it. To calculate it, you simply subtract your expenses from your income. Hopefully you end up with a large positive number. The larger the better! But before you get too excited when you see the number, which is one indicator of net cash flow, remember that this number does not include your loan payment. The loan payment will be determined by how much you pay for the property, your down payment, and the interest rate.

$$NOI\ (Net\ Operating\ Income) =$$
$$Income\ -\ Expenses$$

Income

		Seller Pro Forma	Prior Year Actuals	Our Projected
Gross Scheduled Rent		$48,000		$41,904
Less: Vacancy	7%	$(3,360)		$(2,933)
Net Rental Income		$44,640		$38,971
Plus Other Income		$480		$480
Total Income		$45,120	$41,800	$39,451

Expenses

	Per Unit	Seller Pro Forma	Prior Year Actuals	Our Projected
Repairs and Maintenance	$838	$6,700	$8,010	$8,010
Utilities	$409	$3,273	$3,273	$3,273
Real Estate Taxes	$425	$3,400	$3,400	$3,400
Insurance	$125	$1,000	$1,000	$1,200
Replacement Reserve	$150	$1,200		$1,200
Total Expenses	$1,947/unit	$15,573	$15,683	$17,083
	$2.88/sq. ft.			

Now is the easy part. Take your projected total income of $39,451 and subtract your projected total expenses of $17,083 to get your net operating income of $22,368.

Let's look at NOI a bit closer to portray the full picture:

Net Operating Income

	Seller Pro Forma	Prior Year Actuals	Our Projected
Income Total	$45,120	$41,800	$39,451
(Less) Expense Total	$15,573	$15,683	$17,083
Net Operating Income	$29,547	$26,117	$22,368

This table reveals a brutal fact: the seller's pro forma net operating income is a full $7,179 ($29,547 − $22,368) higher than our projected net operating income. This is a significant difference and would certainly have set up an unsuspecting buyer for failure. I'll say again, net operating income is a very important number, and in a few minutes you'll see why.

Step 4: Find the Capitalization Rate and Valuation

Capitalization rate? I know you're thinking this is starting to sound complicated; definitely third-year college accounting. Well before you close the book, allow me to explain. First, it sounds way more complicated than it is. In numerical terms, the capitalization rate is the net operating income divided by the purchase price.

Capitalization Rate = Net Operating Income ÷ Purchase Price

So now you're thinking, "Ken, how can I calculate the capitalization rate when I don't have a purchase price yet? That's what I'm trying to figure out through this whole exercise after all. Don't tell me algebra is involved!" No, algebra is not involved. This is actually really easy. The purchase price here is actually the purchase price *trends* for a comparable building in your market. So this very complicated sounding word is actually something you can get very easily from brokers, real estate agents, or even the pro forma document for the property. The people in the business—your team members—will either know the capitalization rate for your market or help you calculate it, and that's all there is to it.

To determine how much the property is actually worth—in other words the property's valuation—you just divide the net operating income by the capitalization rate. The number you arrive at is the valuation. It was called purchase price in the previous formula. And the valuation is your initial offer.

Property Value and Offer Price = NOI ÷ Capitalization Rate

So let's continue with our real-world example. The capitalization rate used in the Phoenix property pro forma was 8.74 percent, a standard rate used by the broker. At this stage, I'll just use the capitalization rate provided. There's no point going through a lot of effort to do otherwise until much later, if at all. So we'll divide our NOI by our capitalization rate, and in doing so, we arrive at a property value and offer price of $255,926.

$22,368 ÷ .0874 percent = $255,926
The offer should be no more than
$256,000.

We've arrived! We have an offer price! But there's something missing. Oh, yes, you're probably wondering what the *seller's* asking price was on this property. I won't keep you in suspense. The asking price was $338,000. Of course, you're thinking that sounds really high. Here's an indication of just how high that price is. If you purchased the property with a down payment of 10 percent this would have equated to a loan payment of $25,524 using a 7.5 percent interest rate. Remember our projected net operating income? Let me refresh your memory: it was $22,368. Can you see the problem with this? The income falls well short of even covering your loan, let alone anything else. Had you bought this property at the list price of $338,000 or even at $300,000 you would have been in a negative cash flow situation immediately.

And just in case you're thinking that I pulled our example pro forma from a small-time brokerage company that was unsophisticated, guess again. It was quite the opposite. This pro forma was prepared and distributed by one of the nation's top brokers.

Step 5: Calculate the Loan Payment and Your Profit Cash on Cash

Assuming you and the seller agree to the price of $256,000, now is time to figure out what the loan payment might be. This is where your finance team member or broker could step in, but I did it myself in a matter of seconds. I just went online and typed into my Google search engine the words "mortgage payment," and up popped numerous mortgage calculators. I entered two numbers, the loan amount and the interest rate. Instantaneously the mortgage payment schedule appeared! I love the twenty-first century.

Back to our real-world example. The numbers I used were based on our offer price and 10 percent or $25,600 down and the same interest rate of 7.5 percent. The mortgage calculator churned out a loan payment of $20,010. Certainly a more palatable number when you consider your projected net operating income, which is $22,368.

The very last step is to find out your actual profit by subtracting your loan payment from your projected net operating income. Using the net operating income of $22,368 and subtracting the loan payment of $20,010, the projected profit on this property is $2,358. Is that good or bad? Well here's how you know. You calculate your cash on cash, which you recall, is a lot like return on investment.

To calculate cash on cash, divide your profit of $2,358 by the down payment of $25,600. For this deal, your cash on cash return is 9.2 percent. Not a bad return.

$$Cash\ on\ Cash = Profit \div Down\ Payment$$

Congratulations! If you purchase this property for $256,000 with 10 percent down, your return on investment will be 9.2 percent.

These five steps—the Five Step Property Evaluation—are the most important concepts in this book. They give you the ability to evaluate property investments like the pros do. They give you power and confidence. They give you realistic, fact-based benchmarks to make the best property choices. They give you the basis from which to have reasonable conversations with the seller. And they give you peace of mind that you are not getting into something that may not pan out.

If you spend the time gathering the income and expense information clearly prescribed in this chapter, you'll know what it will take to run this property and how much money you can expect to make from it. You'll be well informed before you even talk to the seller again and certainly before you ever make an offer. I buy all my rental properties this way using these exact same five steps. I would never dream of doing it any other way. I like sleeping at night too much.

CHAPTER 7 ACTION STEPS

- Get on mailing lists to secure several real property pro formas to practice the Five Step Property Evaluation process.

- Use the numbers on the pro forma to calculate your offer price.

- Realize that when you go through these steps for real, you will verify all the numbers on the pro forma with your team members.

- Begin making calls to property owners to discuss buying property you are interested in.

- Perform this valuation process on an actual property with actual data.

The Big Commitment

The last chapter was all about determining the valuation of a property; in essence, building your buying case. The Five Step Property Evaluation is like embarking on a fact-finding mission where you search for the information you need to create a snapshot of the property. I say snapshot, because you really won't know everything there is to know about the property. You'll have a good idea of what the property is all about and a sense of how it got to be that way. You may even have an idea of how it will perform in the future. But you'll know far less than 100 percent of all there is to know. And that's okay. At least the picture is concrete and real, based on numbers and facts. There will be time to find out all the details during the due diligence phase.

Commitments are tough for me anyway. Just ask my wife. Although, thanks to her, I learned many years ago how to recognize a good thing when I saw one. The same is true for property. I've gotten much better at taking the leap toward commitment particularly if I follow one simple rule. When I know 70 percent of everything there is to know about a property, that's enough to make a decision. To me 60 percent is too little, and if I wait until I know 90 percent, someone has either already beaten me to the punch or I fall into the trap of never having enough information to make a decision. As I like to say, analysis paralysis. Looking back I probably didn't know 70 percent of all there was to know about my wife when I made the big commitment. You might say I got lucky. That was marriage. Don't try your luck with real estate.

Before we go any further, I want to point out that if after your analysis you don't think the property is a good investment, in other words, if the net cash flow is too low, then you may need to walk away from the deal or offer a much lower price to make the numbers work. These numbers don't lie and unless your math is wrong, the estimates you arrived at are factual. It is perfectly okay to walk away, although you may feel like you did a lot of work for nothing. But remember, every step in this process is a learning experience, and with every exercise, every calculation, every building walk-through, you are getting smarter. The next time you'll be twice as fast and three times more thorough. Learning is never a waste of time.

I walk away from most deals at this critical point. I make this statement because by now most people are emotionally involved in the property and the process and are reluctant to say no go to a deal. It takes me about thirty minutes to do the Five Step Property Valuation process once I have all the information I need. I use the numbers and my common sense to move to the next deal if the one I'm working on doesn't jibe.

Should you decide the property still looks like a good idea, you'll find your high level of preparation will put you in an excellent position for negotiation because you have all the numbers and all the facts. And believe me, numbers and facts take the emotion right out of the process. But let's be real. There may be some hostility on the part of the seller, who thinks the property is worth far more than you've shown it to actually be; that happens often. But the difference is that armed with the numbers, you are not waltzing into the seller's office making an arbitrary low-ball offer. Instead, you are coming in with a well-prepared case, based on research and facts, calculated with industry-standard formulas, and a realistic offer number. Kick and scream as the seller may, you'll both know that the offer you are presenting is a fair one. It just may take the seller a little longer to arrive at that conclusion.

Now it is time to convince the seller to
sell the property to you.

When you feel good about the numbers and arrive at the decision to buy, you have reached a real milestone. In this phase of the process, the goal is to "tie up the property." What I mean by that is you want to get the property off the market by beginning the process of generating the letter of intent or in some cases executing a purchase and sale contract. As soon as the purchase and sale agreement is signed, the property is no longer available to any other competitive bidders. The quicker you can tie up the property the better chance you have of closing the deal at your price. That's why I try to complete the steps in the last chapter within forty-eight hours of receiving all the necessary information. It's taken me years to get the process that streamlined, but I've also won several deals thanks to our speed.

Regardless of whether it takes you two days or two weeks,

once you make the decision to buy, there is a standard protocol for buying investment property: Remember, the goal is to tie up the property, and during that time, you negotiate the terms of the sale and, equally as important, review the property and its operations in its finest detail. By the time you are done, you may find your offer was too high and needs adjustment. Or you may find it was right on the money. If it is too low, let your own personal ethics be your guide.

Let's get to the protocol. This is typical of larger deals and characteristic of how purchases happen in many states. But every state is different so consult your team members—your attorney, real estate agent, broker—on this one. Regardless of the vehicle, the deal points that you must work through during this protocol are the same. Don't worry so much about the vehicle—whether it's a letter of intent or a standard purchase and sale agreement from the National Association of Realtors—be more aware of the deal points within it.

Letter of Intent

Once you've established the valuation using the five steps in the last chapter, you are ready to draft the letter of intent or a purchase and sale agreement. I prefer to use a standard letter of intent to map out the deal points between myself and the seller before moving to a formal purchase and sale contract. Letters of intent save me a lot of money in attorney fees because attorneys are not usually involved in letters of intent negotiations. Further, the work done during this process makes the actual contract process smoother and faster. The letter of intent contains your offer along with the basic deal points like down payment amount, due diligence time frame, escrow amount, and financing contingencies.

We'll get to contingencies in a minute. But for now you can see why it is a good idea to have your team in place early. The last thing you want to do at this stage of the game is begin relationships with banks, title companies, or investors. You'll want the relationships to be established; time is of the essence. Get your letter of intent out as quickly as possible so you can agree on the basic terms of the deal and tie up the building. In high-demand markets time is not your friend, so I typically fax or pay a courier to hand-deliver the document to the seller. Regular mail is way too slow.

Letters of intent are like a proposal you send to the seller. They are designed to be negotiated and the original document you send over is the starting point. The seller will review the offer and the terms and will usually counter the offer and adjust some of the terms. This is a back-and-forth process, so don't be surprised if it takes weeks to accomplish. That's normal.

Realize, even though you are actively negotiating the terms of the sale with the seller, the property is not off the market. In fact, I recently lost a property during the letter of intent stage. It felt like you can imagine it felt. Unbeknownst to us, the seller was working with another buyer and used our offer to increase the offer of that buyer. The seller ended up completing a purchase and sale agreement with the other buyer and it went into escrow. Not a good feeling! But it happens more often than you think. But don't burn the bridge. This property came back around to us three months later when the first buyer couldn't get financing and we later put the property into escrow.

Sample letters of intent are available on my Web site (www.mc companies.com) and will give you an idea of what these documents look like. They are nothing you need to draft. Typically your real estate broker will prepare letters of intent and you will verify and approve them. Note that the letter of intent is usually not binding. It is just a letter that delineates your intent to purchase the property and the terms of that purchase.

Purchase and Sale Agreement

Once both the buyer and the seller agree upon the terms in the signed letter of intent, you are ready for your attorney to draft up the purchase and sale agreement or you can use a standard form from an agency you may be working with. This is where you communicate all the specifics of the sale, in other words you list exactly what each party is going to do to complete the deal. These can be tens of pages in length and some negotiation takes place here as well. Purchase and sale agreements always spell out how the seller will provide information on the property's current operations. They list critical dates, including when your deposit becomes nonrefundable, when the due diligence evaluation period ends, and your close date. There can be plenty of back-and-forth between the buyer's and the seller's attorneys. But this usually goes much quicker than the letter of intent. That's where the bulk of the deal is hashed out.

When you get ready to actually sign the purchase and sale agreement you will have to put down earnest money, which usually is fully refundable until the completion of the due diligence process and you've secured financing, which we'll talk about later. There is some important language that I make sure is in every contract we sign.

That language is as follows:

- Purchase price: What is the total price?

- Down payment: How much do you need down?

- What is the initial deposit to open escrow and start your detailed research?

- Who holds the buyer's deposit in escrow and when does it become nonrefundable?

- What are the time frames after the agreement acceptance date especially for contingencies and close of escrow date?

- What are the prorations for rents, taxes, insurance, security deposits, all of which should be split between the buyer and seller at close of escrow?

- When will the title report be delivered and what is in it?

- What are the financing contingencies, including getting a new loan or assuming the existing one?

- What are the due diligence time frames, including receipt of all books and records, rental agreements, operating statements, rent rolls, personal property inventories, service contracts, utility information, ALTA* survey, environmental reports, building plans, engineering reports, or any recent appraisals? *As the buyer, you must receive all of these before the due diligence period begins.*

- What is the time frame to perform the pest control inspections?

*An ALTA survey is a boundary survey of your property to reveal the actual property lines and easements.

- What are the time frames for the physical inspections of all interior and exterior spaces, including units and common areas?

- Does the seller have any information with regard to lead-based paint or mold and other allergens?

Again, the contract law governing the sale of commercial property varies by state, so you'll want to make sure you consult a qualified attorney. By now, however, you should have one on your team and he or she should be familiar with your specific goals. Work closely with your attorney and your broker to make sure you receive the items promised in the agreement on time.

Contingencies

Your attorney will be able to advise you about contingencies. Contingencies are provisions within a contract that give you recourse to cancel the deal in the event of unforeseen circumstances. A few examples of typical contingency statements include loan contingencies and due diligence contingencies. These are critical and I recommend they be in every purchase and sale agreement.

A loan contingency states that the sale is contingent on you qualifying for the loan. This gives you an out should the lender refuse to finance the deal. I won't do a contract that doesn't have a loan contingency. We were property-managing a project where a buyer put a deposit of $200,000 in earnest money on a property that didn't have a loan contingency. He didn't get the loan. The sad ending is that he lost his $200,000. True story.

Due diligence contingencies are equally important. This language in a purchase and sale agreement states that you as the buyer are entitled to any and all documents related to the property. It also states that you as the buyer may ask any questions about the property and that you are due answers from the seller to the best of his or her knowledge in a timely manner. As you will come to find out in the next chapter, the results of the due diligence process are ultimately what decides your purchase or decline of the property. They also help you formulate your property plan and operating budget, two steps critical in maximizing your investment. This clause ensures that you get all the information you need.

Signing the Agreement

Once both the buyer and the seller agree upon all the terms of the agreement, you have a completed purchase and sale agreement that is ready to sign and date. This agreement is binding, and in most cases you will be asked to put down an earnest money deposit on the date you sign the contract. Again, this earnest money is fully refundable and you can walk away from the deal until you have completed and waived the contingencies such as due diligence and getting the loan. And that's what we'll cover in the next chapter.

But as binding as the agreement is, with the right language built in you can walk away, extend your dates, or adjust your offer based on your findings during due diligence. We have rescinded our offers on a few properties for just cause. In fact there was one property that we pursued through the signing of the purchase and sale agreement. During the due diligence investigation process, the structural engineer on our team found that the building was built on what they term in Arizona "expansive soil." What that means is that the soil expands and contracts more than normal and can cause foundation problems. Knowing that, we looked further and found a twenty-foot hairline crack in the pool, small foundation cracks, and exterior wall separations. This was indicative of bigger problems that could be incredibly costly, and we felt the risk was too great, so we sent a letter to the seller stating that we were rescinding our purchase offer in accordance with the terms of the agreement.

CHAPTER 8 ACTION STEPS

- Visit my Web site (www.mccompanies.com) and print out several sample letters of intent and get familiar with the provisions and language.

- Do the same with purchase and sale agreements.

- Continue to seek out property prospects, calculate valuation, and when you see a deal with numbers that work, generate a real letter of intent or in some states the purchase and sale agreement.

Chapter 9

Due Diligence:
The Easter Egg Hunt

In Webster's dictionary, the definition of "diligent" is "prosecuted with careful attention and effort." But it's really the synonyms for the word that reveal exactly what is expected during the due diligence period when purchasing investment real estate. The synonyms for "diligent" include "conscientious, thorough, careful, thoughtful, attentive, and meticulous." And that's exactly how you need to behave when you do due diligence on a property. You need to conscientiously review every document pertaining to property operations. You need to perform thorough walk-throughs of every apartment unit. You need to pay careful attention to every detail. You need to be thoughtful about how you can improve the property and cut expenses. You need to be attentive to the tasks and deliver them on time and you need to be meticulous in your evaluation and reporting.

Thanks, Webster, I couldn't have said it better myself. And that's really what the due diligence process is. It is your time to take a thorough look at everything pertaining to the property and report the good, the bad, and the ugly. It's the time when you make detailed assessments of actual costs for property improvements, ongoing maintenance, and operations. It's your last chance to make sure you have uncovered every hidden flaw, are aware of every possible problem, and are realistically projecting the opportunities.

> *The goal of due diligence is to find out*
> *100 percent of everything there is to*
> *know about the property and*
> *generate an operating plan and*
> *budget from that information.*

In my years of buying property, I've uncovered everything imaginable during due diligence. In one building, while doing a thorough unit-by-unit walk-through, I found everything from vacant units that were supposed to be occupied (falsified rent rolls), units that cannot be leased because fixtures have been removed to repair other leased apartments (cannibalized units), a loose ten-foot-long boa constrictor left behind by a resident, a naked man in what should have been a vacant unit, roof damage so bad I could see daylight, innumerable missing appliances, units missing carpeting, you name it.

You'll be surprised by what you find. Or in some cases, you won't be surprised at all. But either way, you'll rest much easier after the whole process is over and you know the property you are purchasing has been fully revealed to you. You'll be loving the language in your purchase and sale agreement that says all units must be rent-ready at close of escrow!

Right now you're probably thinking there are a thousand things to look at related to a property. This would take a year to accomplish. You're right, there are a lot of things to look at and evaluate, but you're wrong about the timetable. The bad news is you don't have a year to accomplish the due diligence. Rather, you typically have about thirty days. Eeeek! That's impossible! I thought that too, but then I remembered, I have a team, and they can make the due diligence process much easier, way more manageable, and actually a good time.

To me due diligence is really kind of fun. I guess it's the element of surprise and of finding the unexpected—both for the good and the bad. It's like an Easter egg hunt, and come to think of it, as a kid, I used to like those too. You just never know what you are going to find. But unlike my preparation for an Easter egg hunt I come to the due diligence process with more than an Easter basket. In all cases, because I was thorough on the initial property valuation, I have a strong belief that whatever I find is fixable. I also take comfort in knowing that anything I find that would cost me money to fix is a final negotiation point before the sale closes. That's right: If you find that the property requires any type of major repair, such as a new roof, exterior painting, new appliances, termite extermination, snake and naked man removal, you can get estimates and factor the costs into the final valuation and purchase price. That's what I call finding the golden egg!

The Due Diligence Checklist

As I mentioned, I've gotten really good at due diligence. I've seen it all and our due diligence checklist is compiled from over fifteen years of experience. For years, every time we thought we had everything on the list, we'd encounter a property that would throw us a curve. For the past year or so, this checklist has remained static. We really feel we've got it all.

The Due Diligence Checklist

The File Audit
Purpose: To verify the actual potential income calculation.

Look for:

- A signed rental agreement on every unit to ensure you have binding contracts.
- Monthly rental rates from the rent roll that match the numbers used in your offer.
- Security deposits that match the amounts reported to the escrow agent. They belong to the residents, so they transfer to the new owners.
- The quality of the residents in each unit. Do they pay on time? Are they creating problems for other residents? Have credit background and criminal checks been completed on all residents?

The Interior Inspection

Purpose: To help you learn about the physical property, get a sense of the quality of the residents, and help you understand the exposure to your future cash flow should you purchase the property. You'll determine the actual condition of the personal property and get a feel for the extent of major repairs.

Look for:

- Clues about the lifestyles of the current residents. I've witnessed everything from major drug activity to people living in squalor. Think about what you are seeing. A resident living without furniture, sleeping on the floor, and keeping his articles in a Hefty bag could be a future vacancy.

- Residents not living in units that the seller had designated as rented. Some sellers inflate their rent rolls and list residents who don't really exist, or simply have such bad records that they do not know the current rental picture.

- Missing furniture, appliances, or items near the end of their useful life. Make a list of all appliances, carpet, vinyl floors, and cabinets that fall into these categories.

- Major water, fire, or resident damage to the premises and contents.

- Telltale signs of pest problems in each unit and document any pest control needs.

Government Agency Reviews

Purpose: To determine that the property is in compliance with government standards.

Look for:

- Fire code violations. I invite the local fire department to complete an inspection. This inspection with our Portland project discovered an old fire sprinkler system in need of repair that even the current owners didn't know about.

- Outstanding permit problems. Have any remodels, additions, pools, and so forth been added without proper permitting?

- Environmental concerns such as asbestos, mold, lead paint, or radon.

- Existing ownership issues like zoning violations or encroachment onto another property.

Service Agreement Review

Purpose: To determine the service commitments of the current owner and look for ways to improve them should they survive a transfer of ownership.

Look for:

- Pool service agreements.

- Heating, air conditioning, and cooling service agreements.

- Landscaping contracts.

- Coin-op laundry equipment service contracts.

- Cable and alarm contracts.
- Parking contracts.
- Advertising contracts.

Exterior Inspections

Purpose: To evaluate all exterior components of the property and determine when they may need repair or replacement.

Look for:

- Roof problems, including signs of leaks and overall disrepair or wear.
- The condition of heating, ventilation, and cooling systems and the equipment service and maintenance records. What is the repair history and the age of each piece of equipment?
- Electrical wiring that is not in compliance with current codes.
- Plumbing that is aged, corroded, or leaking and the type of plumbing. Copper, PVC, and galvanized plumbing all have their own unique problems.
- The condition of the exterior paint and trim.
- The condition of the driveways and parking lots. Are they cracking and full of potholes? What repairs are necessary?
- Landscaping problems, including irrigation and sprinkler system breaks, large trees that need trimming, and root growth that is cracking sidewalks or causing foundation problems.

The purpose of this entire inspection process is to put an estimated cost to each item in the list. Not simply for cost sake but to arrive at a total number that we can take back to the seller and discuss. What if the property is not in compliance with the fire department? What if there are environmental hazards? What if three out of the eight units obviously need new carpeting? In many cases, if you bring these issues to the seller's attention, they can be fixed before you close. That saves you money—in some cases, lots of it.

Books and Records

As important as it is to know everything about the physical property, you absolutely need to dig just as deep into its operations. That means looking at the books and records. This is also the time to begin gathering information for your operating budget by categorizing the income and expenses. These are the things I review in great detail:

• Twenty-four months of income and expense statements: I compare the income and expenses to the projections. This is the time to make notes for the operating budget and flush out all the unusual expenses or major periods of rent loss. Discuss these with your seller or broker *before* the due diligence period ends. You absolutely want to meet your deadlines.

• All service agreements: I look for those agreements with termination clauses longer than thirty days. I verify that these costs are in the operating budget, whether the service is needed, and also what services are missing. I assess the current management company and determine whether they stay or go. I review all advertising agreements for effectiveness. It's worth your time to look at all these agreements because you could find yourself locked into them. Any contract you don't want to assume, you need to spell it out before the completion of due diligence.

• Current rent roll: This is when I verify the actual income, the actual potential income, and the future potential income to the penny. Take a hard look at every unit that is under the market rent. This is your golden egg "Advance to Boardwalk" card that will create an increase in your cash flow after you purchase the property. Take detailed notes for your management plan and operating budget.

• Utility bills: Here I verify all the utilities. Call the utility companies and get the last twelve months' operating history on each account. Ask about increases for the next year. Finally, insert the revised figures into your budget.

• Payroll information: On larger properties I look at who is working at the property and how much they are paid, especially if I want them to stay and work for me or the management company. When assuming these employees, treat them like new hires. Be sure to find out the accrued vacation information. We also run a criminal and credit background checks on all new hires as well as complete a drug screening before we acquire them.

For me the due diligence process is an exciting time. Sure I get some great stories out of what I see, but more importantly, I know that whatever I find will be documented for the next round of discussions with the seller. The due diligence document is my report card to evaluate how well I estimated the numbers during the Five Step Property Evaluation. In many cases the problems I find during due diligence either result in a reduction in the price of the property or, better yet, they are fixed before we close escrow.

It's this kind of information that is only going to help you be more successful with whatever property you purchase—this one or another. We recently found a new landscape company in this way. I received a monthly landscape contract on a property we were considering. The landscaping looked great and I was surprised to see the cost was much lower than what I was paying at some of my other properties. In fact, it was lower than what I budgeted for this project! This one find is saving me thousands because now this landscaping company does the bulk of our work at this and our other properties.

Regardless of whether I find hidden jewels like a great landscape company I didn't know about before, or buried warts that if missed would have negatively impacted cash flow, I am happy. Happy because additional revenue opportunities are always great and happy because any problems now in the open give me additional bargaining leverage. Only the stuff that isn't found during due diligence is scary to me.

Once the sale is closed, you're stuck with any and all hidden problems. And they can cost a lot. Imagine not checking the property's drainage only to find that after a big rainstorm raw sewage drained into one or more of your apartments. Don't laugh, it happened to a friend of mine on Maui. And the costs to clean up all the damage and correct the drainage problem were huge. That's why, as you can imagine, I am very diligent during due diligence. You should be too.

CHAPTER 9 ACTION STEPS

- Review the detailed Due Diligence Checklist and make copies of it so you can use it as a guide as you are inspecting properties.

- Use your team members to help with the inspections and to ensure you meet your due diligence deadlines.

- Look for and keep notes of golden eggs—management plan opportunities you see when you look at the property and analyze the books.

- Categorize income and expense items as you discover them for the development of your operating budget.

- Stay calm about problems you find. Remember, if you find them during due diligence, the expense of taking care of them will not come out of your wallet.

- Be keenly aware of and adhere to the critical dates in the contract.

Chapter 10

Making Sense of It All

Now that you have all the information, how do you make sense of it all and know what to look for. You may feel you've just become part of the research business instead of the property investment business. And at some point you're going to want to get out of analysis mode and say "Show me the money."

This chapter will show you how to make sense of all the data, and how to put it into a form that will enable you to see exactly where the money-making opportunities are and where they aren't. Because remember, at this point, you are still in due diligence mode, so if you find that the money-making opportunities aren't there, there is still time to renegotiate the purchase price or pull out of the deal entirely if the numbers simply won't add up to profit in your pocket.

In the sections that follow, I'll walk you through how to formulate a management plan and an operating budget simultaneously for the property. They really go hand in hand. The management plan will define the key strategies you will use to either cut expenses, increase income, or both. The operating budget links numbers to those strategies and helps you quantify your bang for the buck.

At this point, I ask myself how I will run the property once it's mine. I'd rather take the time before I've closed on the sale to develop a few "what if" scenarios than to live through some "if only" scenarios: "If only I had taken the time to develop an operating budget. If only I had bothered to hire a property manager to help me assess the cost of maintenance." If only, if only. The goal of this chapter is to make sure you never say "if only."

Why Go It Alone?

This is a critical juncture. You'll want to call in your team to help you or even just provide their opinions on the data you compiled. I typically call in my tax accountant, property management expert, insurance agent, contractors, and anyone else who I may need to make a thorough evaluation.

Not long ago, we were in due diligence on a property in Tucson, Arizona, that was in bad need of repair. There was no way I could estimate the costs of repairs on my own, as they were way beyond the scope of my expertise. So I called in my contractor to do a site inspection and asked him what it would take to get the place in shape. He provided me with a rough estimate of $700,000, which we provided the seller.

Unfortunately the Tucson property had been severely neglected and the seller, which was the bank, was not interested in making the needed repairs. They were also not interested in entertaining our greatly reduced purchase price. So we parted ways and moved on to the next deal. Even though we didn't close on the property, the information was out in the open, and that's the power. There are no strong-arm tactics here, just the reality. And the reality was I wasn't buying the property at my initial offer price knowing it needed $700,000 in repairs.

The Property Plan—Adding Value

It would be nice if making sense of your property evaluation was as easy as finding that $700,000 worth of repairs are needed, saying, Mr. Seller, we want to reduce our asking price by $700,000, take it or leave it. It's not that simple. With the Tucson property, we looked at the $700,000 repair bill as part of the bigger picture. And that bigger picture is called the property plan.

You will reach your financial goals much quicker if you can find property that is underperforming and kick it into shape through sound management. As you probably know by now, sound management means reducing expenses and raising income. That's how you increase the value of your investment. Hopefully, during your evaluation and due diligence you found some specific ways to increase the cash flow of the property. Here's some food for thought:

- While walking the property, did you turn the corner and ask where the laundry facility is only to be told there isn't one?

- Did you walk into one of the units and find a breathtaking mountain view and later look on the rent roll to discover there was no premium for this unit?

- During your property inspection, did you encounter a ramshackle tennis court that would be an ideal location for six more rental units or garages?
- Have you thought about investing $20,000 to install access gates, which increase the perceived value of the property and enable you to add $10 or $15 in rent per unit, per month?

You get the idea. The property itself should be showing *you* the money. If you aren't seeing increased income potential around almost every corner, you're not looking very hard—or there may not be much. If it's the latter, you may want to consider another property alternative.

Your team members should be active participants in your mission of finding income-generating or expense-saving opportunities. They will see things you don't see. If you think there is no creativity in this business, you are dead wrong. I have more fun walking properties with my team and just exploring the possibilities. Remember, that's how money is made—when you and your team see things other people don't see and then capitalize on them.

At this point, your job is to ask "what if?" And with every "what if," enter the numbers into the budget and see how the bottom line shapes up. Here are a few what if's you should be asking of the properties you are considering:

- What if I increase the rents?
  - Will it create more vacancy?
  - How quickly will I rent the unit if someone moves out?
  - Can I test it on vacant units before issuing increases to existing residents?

- What is the market rent in the area and are my rents in line with the market?

- What if I need to attract new residents?

  - Do I have a system in place?
  - Do I have a waiting list if I am full?
  - Am I keeping in touch with the vacancy rates and concessions in the area by communicating with my team and surveying competitors regularly?
  - Is that advertisement in the newspaper worth the expense and is it making my telephone ring and getting me rentals?
  - What is the advertising cost per rental?

- What if I plan to adhere to the lease agreement?

  - Will it generate more income through late fees, nonsufficient funds fees, parking fees, water and sewer fees?
  - If I do this what does it mean financially?
  - Will it create more vacancies?

- What if I charged location premiums, installed access gates, or put in a children's play area?

  - Would the residents pay for it?
  - What other things can I provide that the residents will pay for?
  - Will the investment pay for itself within twenty-four months?

- What if I replace an item instead of repair it?

  - How much more rent will I get?

- What if I bid out my landscaping and maintenance and repairs?

  - Would I save any money?

- What if I had a couple of insurance companies bid my insurance?

  ○ Would I save any money?

- What if I installed energy-efficient lighting?

  ○ How much would it cost?
  ○ How much money would I save in energy bills?
  ○ Would the return on investment be worth the outlay of cash?

- What if I hire my own maintenance person to handle routine maintenance?

  ○ How many repairs can my maintenance person handle?
  ○ How often am I paying for an outside service to do routine maintenance?
  ○ What can I personally do to save money? Property management, landscaping, accounting, painting the units on move-out, cleaning them before the next person moves in?
  ○ Do I really know my property so that if an unusual expense shows up I recognize and can flag or investigate it?

As you can see, there are lots of ways to increase income and reduce expenses. It just takes looking at the property and seeing the opportunities, understanding the residents' needs, and creatively coming up with solutions.

Real-World Example

My partner and I recently purchased a 182-unit property located in Sun City, Arizona, an age-restricted fifty-five-and-older community. It was constructed in 1996 and was in excellent condition. The ownership was based in New York City and this was their only property in Arizona. After running the numbers we calculated that the property was worth about $9 million based on the prior two years' actual operating numbers. This property was never listed for sale.

We tied the property up at $9 million and started the due diligence process. We revised our operating budget for future operations while we developed the property plan. Through all our investigation, we discovered three main areas that were ripe for better management under new ownership:

1. Transportation: The existing residents wanted some sort of community transportation.
2. Apartment location: The seniors at this community didn't like to climb stairs, so the upstairs apartments were usually the ones that were vacant.
3. Cable and alarm: The property was locked into a bulk rate cable and alarm agreement.

After doing our research in the surrounding area we found that we were one of the only communities without a van to shuttle the residents around the community, to and from appointments and special events. We found that our competition had transportation service and had a much higher occupancy because the van service attracted seniors who didn't want to drive. With that knowledge, we budgeted $54,000 for a twenty-one-person van into our operational projections. We have owned this property long enough to tell you that this investment in the van has increased our rentals, occupancy, and cash flow and ultimately the property value.

The second action we took in response to the three items in our plan related to pricing. Clearly our residents valued the first-floor apartments more than the second-floor units, so we priced them accordingly, making the first-floor rents slightly higher than the second-floor rents. Over time we were able to lease these first-floor apartments for $75 per month higher than the second-floor apartments. We also increased the rent on the units that had exceptionally good locations or outstanding views. This equated to over a $6,000-per-month increase in our cash flow and the first-floor apartments are still 100 percent occupied!

Finally, in response to point three in our plan, we renegotiated the bulk cable and alarm agreements. The existing agreements combined were about $21 per unit per month for all 182 apartments, regardless of whether or not the apartment was occupied. This equated to a $3,822 per month savings. Better yet, the residents liked the new arrangement because for the first time they could choose the cable plan they wanted, instead of being locked into a plan negotiated by the absentee ownership eight years prior. The same went for alarm service.

I know you're thinking that, wow, it must be great to have all that extra income every month from simply executing this plan, and you're right, it absolutely is. But the benefit of good operations goes one further. Remember from earlier in this book: The value of a multi-unit rental property is a function of operations. Well, the result of all this increased operating income paid off just as we had planned: in a recent appraisal of $11.3 million, over $2 million more than we paid for the property just one year ago. This is the power of planning your success and using a good property management company that can, first, identify new ways to increase the net operating income and that, second, has the experience to help you make it happen. This in turn increases the value of the property and increases the return to investors.

I can't emphasize enough the importance of putting your property plan on paper and then working your plan. It is not a complicated document. There's no need to put it in a big three-ring binder. As you can see, the property plan that yielded us thousands of dollars in operating income and millions in appraised property value was a simple three-point plan.

The property plan is simply your goal for the property. And just as I stated earlier in this book that you need to tell everyone you see and know about your own personal goal, you need to do the same here. You should communicate the goal you have for the property to your property managers, your investors, and perhaps most of all, yourself.

At this point, we've done a great job of finding all the opportunities and all the hidden expenses. We have some great ideas for inclusion in our property plan. But for all this work, we still only have words on a page. We need to make the leap to the numbers side of things. So, take a deep breath, leave your college accounting phobias behind, and let's do it.

The Operating Budget

This really sounds much more complicated than it is. In Chapter 7 I taught you how to read a seller's pro forma and make an offer. The steps to the budget are not all that different. You calculate the property income by using the information you obtained on the income statement, rent survey, rent roll, and operating statements. Then you look at expenses based on the actual and projected expenses you've gleaned from the due diligence process.

Let's look at income first and revisit some of our concepts in a new light.

ACTUAL POTENTIAL INCOME

The main source of income on most any property is usually the rent existing residents are paying. That's the actual potential income of the property. For that reason, you'll want your rent figures to be as accurate as possible based on the information that you have. The easiest way to get this information is to get the existing rent roll or schedule of what each resident is paying, put the units in numerical order, and add up the rent amounts. Another way is to physically review each lease at the property and write down the rent each occupant is paying and mark off all vacant units. It's a good idea to do this anyway just to make sure that all the residents listed have binding lease agreements.

Once your analysis is completed, your spreadsheet should look something like this:

Apt #	Type of Unit	Size / sq. ft.	Monthly Rent	Resident
Unit 1	1 bedroom	650	$410	Kiyosaki
Unit 2	1 bedroom	650	$410	Hopkins
Unit 3	1 bedroom	650	$410	Beckel
Unit 4	1 bedroom	**650**	**$430**	**VACANT**

Unit 5	1 bedroom	650	$425	McCallister
Unit 6	1 bedroom	650	$420	Flanagan
Unit 7	2 bedroom	750	$490	Lechter
Unit 8	2 bedroom	750	$470	Stullick
Total		**5,400**	**$3,492**	

Based on this rent roll, the actual potential income *including the vacant unit* is $3,492 per month. Use this number as your actual potential income in your budget.

OTHER INCOME OPPORTUNITIES

Most properties have other income opportunities. These should also be factored into your budget. The most common examples of other income budget items include the following:

- Laundry income.
- Parking income.
- Water and sewer income.
- Late fees.
- Nonsufficient funds fees.
- Cable income.
- Internet revenue.
- Telephone income.

From the operating statements and individual ledger cards for each resident you should get an idea of what other types of income exist at the property. After all, somebody has to deposit this money into the bank account, so there is a paper trail somewhere.

Sometimes this information is difficult to get from the seller. Not everyone is a good bookkeeper. If this is the case with the property you are buying, you will need to re-create the records from the facts you do know. For example, if there is a laundry room with coin-operated washers and dryers and you do not see the laundry income on the seller's income and expense statements, you will need to go directly to the company that services the machines and collects the coins to find out how much you should expect on a monthly basis.

Finding the other income sources can take some time. Kim Kiyosaki just told me recently that she was buying a property from a seller whose books showed that for over four years the laundry company had not paid anything to the sellers. The washers and dryers were there. People were using them. You can bet this detail was flushed out during due diligence and a realistic income number was entered into an operating budget before Kim bought the property.

This is the process of uncovering and entering onto a spreadsheet your income opportunities. Each opportunity should have its own line. Once you have exhausted all the existing income opportunities, you enter lines for any new income opportunities you may add once you take over the property. With income out of the way, you do just as we did before when we were valuing the property, you turn to the expenses.

Expenses

Just as you created a new line for each income opportunity for your property, you'll create a new line item in your spreadsheet for each expense. In the sections that follow, I'll list and describe most of the most typical expenses you will encounter with your new property.

PAYROLL

Payroll covers the salaries and wages you pay yourself or your staff. A typical management staff, depending on the size of the property, can include several people. First there are the on-site managers and leasing agents. Then there's the housekeeping staff that assist with unit turnover and upkeep of common areas. There are also maintenance people who complete minor repairs of buildings and grounds. Again, the property management expert on your team can tell you how much management and maintenance you can expect and the kinds of costs you'll incur. In addition to the actual wages for yourself and your staff, if you have one, you'll want to factor in state and federal taxes, worker's compensation, health and dental insurance, as well as possibly a 401(k) plan.

ADMINISTRATIVE

Administrative costs include the fees you pay for special professional services such as an attorney to help you establish partnerships and assist you with evictions. Accountants will help you manage accounts receivable and accounts payable as well as guide you through tax laws and tax reporting. If you plan to manage the property yourself, your accountant will come in handy. In addition to these professional services, all the things you do to run the property on a day-to-day basis are considered administrative expenses. These include everything from Post-it notes and postage stamps to criminal and credit background checks.

MARKETING AND ADVERTISING

You can ask the property owner to show you the advertising costs for the past year and you may or may not get usable information. Better than that, ask the management company representative to give you an estimate of projected costs to advertise the property. He or she will know all the advertising vehicles in your market, the costs, and have a good feel for just how competitive the market is. You should know that as well, but the management company will put those abstractions into marketing dollars. The more competitors there are in your market, the more you need to advertise to get noticed. That costs more money.

MANAGEMENT COSTS

Management costs include the fees you pay to a professional management company or the salaries and wages you pay to yourself or your own staff. Again, when you meet with your property management representative, this person can give you insight on how much your management fees will be, what maintenance costs you can expect, and the nature of those costs.

REPAIR AND MAINTENANCE COSTS

Repair and maintenance expenses will vary depending on your unit turnover or how many move-outs and move-ins you experience in a given year. Other factors that affect repair and maintenance costs are your resident profile, property condition, and the responsiveness of the manager to resident repair requests. If you keep your property in top condition, you will spend less in the long run on things like carpet cleaning, interior painting, electrical repairs, plumbing, appliance repairs, heating and air conditioning repairs and service. Landscaping, pool service and supplies, and pest control also fall under this category.

PROPERTY TAXES

There are two kinds of property taxes: real property taxes, which are on the real estate property, and personal property taxes, which are taxes on the contents of the property like refrigerators, stoves, dishwashers, and other appliances. There are two ways to get these numbers. First they are typically listed on the financials you receive from the owner, or you can get them from the tax assessor's office. One thing to know is that taxes usually go up after you purchase the property because the assessors use the new purchase price as the new assessed value. Yet another reason to make sure you don't overpay for the property! So when you are entering in the property tax costs into your analysis, you may want to inflate them. Your property tax team member can give you insight on how much to raise the tax costs.

INSURANCE

This is an important line item expense and it's a critical one. Why? First, insurance is expensive, and second because usually the bank requires you to have insurance locked and loaded before signing the loan. This number is easy to get. Just call up a few insurance agents and get some quotes. The kind of insurance you will need includes property/casualty and general liability. Deductibles are what will make your insurance costs vary. We vary our deductibles depending on the property. As a rule, you'll want to have insurance for the big things that can go wrong. You don't want to pay high premiums for all the small things that you could afford to pay out of pocket. Talk with your insurance agent about the proper coverage for your property and the risks of having high deductibles.

UTILITIES

Identify all the utilities used in the building. This can include electric, gas, trash, sewer, water, cable, and phone. Check to see if the utilities are individually metered, which means each rental unit has its own meter, or if the utilities are master-metered. If they are master-metered, there is one meter for the entire building. Individually metered is the better scenario because the resident pays their own bills. Individually metered buildings mean lower expenses to you because every resident pays for their own utilities. In master-metered buildings there is no incentive for the tenants to keep utility costs down.

I stay clear of buildings that are master-metered for this very reason. Ask the owner to provide you with the financials for the property and these numbers should be there, but again, I always verify them. To verify the figures all you need is the building address and the utility companies can supply you the bills for the previous year. If they won't disclose the information, call the owner and ask him or her to contact the utility company and authorize the release. Be sure to get all the bills. Sometimes there are seasonal differences, especially for heating and air conditioning. Let's not have any surprises!

CAPITAL REPAIRS

These are the major improvements needed to keep or bring the property up to standard. Often properties in need of some work are the best buying opportunities, but you'll want to have a realistic assessment of just how much money it will take to get the place livable and looking good. I'm talking repairs to roofs, parking areas, sidewalks, driveways, lighting, and purchases of carpeting, appliances, hot water heaters, air conditioners, and so on. This is all the stuff you would look at when buying a home—except you're evaluating it on a much bigger scale.

When you finish entering all the expenses into your operating budget, total the income and total the expenses. Subtract the expenses from the income and you will get a good picture of your cash flow and net operating income. If it's really big, go back and make sure your calculations are correct. And if it's negative, don't be discouraged. This is where creative accounting comes in. Not the kind that will land you in a white-collar-crimes prison, but the kind that makes you reassess your business model.

Once the budget is finished you'll want to compare it to the actual operating income and expenses of your property and look for any glaring errors or omissions. If you have tried every which way to make the bottom line a positive number or, let's face it, a number that you're happy with and the deal still isn't working, you may want to consult with your team. If you've exhausted their ideas or the ideas they have presented are so far-fetched, you may have to lower the offer price further or simply walk away from the deal if you can't realize a positive cash flow or a cash flow you will be satisfied with. The last thing you'd want to do is move forward and pray for a miracle. That's not how miracles work. Lucky breaks come to those who do their homework and through preparedness recognize opportunities.

Confrontation Time

This doesn't have to be difficult, but you do eventually have to reveal to the seller your findings on the property. And you'll need to do this before the end of due diligence or the property is yours, warts and all, as the saying goes.

It's all in the presentation. You can ram your findings down the seller's throat, plant your feet in the sand, and say, "Take it or leave it." Better yet, take a tactful, matter-of-fact approach that attacks neither the property nor the seller's ego. It is a discussion about the numbers, not about the seller's or the buyer's honesty and integrity. It's a direct conversation about the numbers where everything is out on the table and there are no underlying motives.

There are times, yes, when there can be blatant seller cover-ups. But in most instances, as was my experience with our Portland project, the seller has no idea how much money is needed for repairs or maintenance, for instance. You are the bearer of that news, so it is in your best interest to do it professionally, truthfully, and with documentation.

The property plan process and your professionalism can help you avoid the swift kick out the door, and best of all, help you create a win-win final property negotiation. After all, you should not be trying for the win-lose scenario. You never want to burn bridges in this business. Your seller today could be your buyer tomorrow or even lead you to your next deal. I've had plenty of instances where a seller on one deal has turned into an investor on another deal or a seller on another building. I never lose sight of the fact that this is a relation-ship business.

Here is a short reference list of findings I've had to confront sellers with in the past; you may find yourself in the same position:

- Vacant units listed as occupied on the rent roll.

- Notices to vacate or unreported future vacancies.

- Poor resident profiles with high credit risk that could create future vacancy.

- Missing appliances, carpet, and so forth—somebody has to pay for this.

- High maintenance expenses required to get the units in rent-ready condition.

- Pest control issues, including termites, scorpions, roaches, and pigeons.

- Noncancelable service contracts that add expense to your operating budget and affect your cash flow.

- Utility costs much higher than the previous year.

- Prior insurance loss at the property that affects the cost of future insurance.

- Property tax higher than disclosed.

- Violation notices from the city.

- Fire code violations.

- Environmental problems.

Moving Forward

The operating budget is the last big test of a property's worthiness. If the operating budget calculations look good for the first year and you project that you will make enough money to achieve your goal, you are ready to move forward and take ownership of the property. Remember, you will likely be adjusting the offer price slightly to account for any repairs, upkeep, improvements, or other costs you may have discovered during due diligence. Present your numbers and your rationale to the seller and finish the deal.

It was a long time coming, from initial market evaluation, to property search, to selection, to property evaluation, and finally to developing an operating budget. You will soon be the proud owner of investment rental property. Now the thrill of ownership begins. It's time to execute your plan to improve the property and maximize its cash flow. That is the subject of our next chapter.

CHAPTER 10 ACTION STEPS

- Visit www.mccompanies.com to download the chart of accounts and sample budgets.

- List all your projected expenses and income sources for your budget.

- Enter the projected numbers for each expense and each income source.

- Total the spreadsheet and perform similar calculations on several "what if" scenarios:

  - increased/decreased expenses
  - increased/decreased income

- Determine the expense and income levels that maximize cash flow.

- Make that the foundation for your property plan.

Chapter 11

You Own It . . .
Now What?

Congratulations! You're the proud owner of real estate investment property. After the toasts are over and you've finished calling your spouse, mom, and dad to let them know the deal has gone through, you'll sit back, relax, and in about five minutes, you'll probably think . . . now what? Unless you have a plan, which of course, you do.

You may be amazed to discover that I have never purchased a single property without going through the process described in the last chapters. To me it has just never seemed worth the risk to rely on gut instincts alone. And I certainly do everything in my power to not get emotionally attached to any property. In fact, I go into every property deal with the full assumption that I won't close the sale. That sounds pessimistic perhaps, and anyone who knows me, knows I am an optimist through and through. So what's with the negativity?

I don't really look at it as negativity. I look at my attitude as realism. No one likes to work harder than they have to, including me. And I know through personal experience and through the stories of hundreds of people who have shared their struggles with me at Rich Dad Seminars, there is no fix, no repair, no advertising strategy that can mend a property that you simply paid too much for. Even improved management practices don't do the trick.

I hope you realize that no matter how many deals I do, I still go through the same valuation process, the same contract process, the same due diligence process, and perhaps most important the same property planning process. I don't take shortcuts and, knock on wood, I have not had one property that has not performed. Some may look at what I do and say, "The guy must love risk." But in truth, I don't feel that what I do is risky at all. Doing the homework helps create sure things. Or as close as anyone can get to sure things. It has paid off for me.

By now you know I don't leave much to chance, and buying an apartment building without a solid plan of how I am going to increase income and reduce expenses to maximize my cash flow is not going to happen. Through much of the work you will have completed so far, you should have solid ideas in your plan for how to run your building. That's great. Now's the time to put those ideas in motion. This is not a drill. I repeat. This is not a drill.

Follow Through

Follow through. Those are words that will become our mantra for this chapter, because in the pages ahead, I'll walk you through managing the property. Before you think that we'll be talking about shampooing carpets and trimming trees, let me clarify that managing the property means following through on your property plan and staying within your operating budget. Managing the property is about maximizing your cash flow.

At this point, you may have already decided to manage the property yourself or to hire a professional management company. I know plenty of people in both camps and they all say the same thing. It is simply a matter of choosing how you want to spend your time. I know one property owner who is incredibly successful. He has vacation homes in some of the most beautiful places on earth. He owns apartment buildings, we manage them, but he does all his own painting. Sure it saves him a ton of money, but it's more than that. I think it's being part of management that he really enjoys.

Property Manager Job Description

Regardless of whether you decide to hire outside management or do it yourself, you'll want to make sure you know either what kind of job you've just created for yourself or what you expect of the property management company you hire. So think of this chapter as either what to look for in a property management company or what to expect of yourself as your own property manager.

The key to good property management and a good property manager has to do with systems. Systems to handle advertising and marketing, leasing, employee-related issues, hiring of outside vendors and bidding for services, reporting, emergencies, maintenance requests, rent collection, accounting, operating budgets, legal procedures, and anything else necessary for running rental property.

Not only must a property manager have all these systems in place, he or she must follow them.

The tasks of a property manager fall into several categories:

SOLVING PROBLEMS DAILY

The main function of a property manager is first and foremost to implement your property plan, and second to solve problems. This is what I do every day with my property management company. My staff and I handle thousands of units combined and even though our job title says property manager, we are really problem solvers. Because the reality of the business is that you are managing a lot less than you are problem solving, especially in the beginning when you just take over a property.

HANDLING STAFFING ISSUES

Property managers also handle all staffing issues. If you need a leasing agent on site, the property management company will have trained and qualified professionals to handle the job. If you are doing it yourself, either you or someone you hire will take on the task. That means you'll be responsible for training and equipping the person you hire with all the knowledge, skills, and materials he or she will need for success. This can include training in customer service, sales, fair housing policies, and so on.

You'll also need a maintenance person or handyman. Again, this may be you or it may be someone you hire. If you contract with a property management company, they will usually provide this service. If you are managing the property yourself, look for a person who has enough time and who will be available to you anytime you call. The last thing you want is a resident with a leaky water pipe or a clogged toilet waiting for service. It's damaging to your property as well as to your reputation. An angry resident will move out and not only leave you with a vacant non-income-producing problem, that angry resident will cost you money to get the unit back into rent-ready condition.

LEASING THE PROPERTY

It is the property manager's job to do the advertising required to keep the property at 100 percent occupancy or as close to it as possible. That means knowing which advertising vehicles get results and developing the promotions and promotional messages that get the job done. This could be ads, it could be signs, it could be signing agreements with local apartment finder services, or it could be setting up a resident referral program. There are an unlimited number of tactics for getting prospective resident traffic. Professional property management companies know what works and what doesn't. You can also handle this part of the job on your own.

But be aware that getting residents is not the sole objective. You want to attract the right residents. So as a rule, I never rent an apartment to anyone who has not been run through a criminal and credit check. In every apartment building or community that we manage, every applicant is run through a background check. We are not under any obligation by law to rent to criminals or sex offenders under any equal housing act. And I don't feel any moral obligation to give those who need a "fresh start" a home in our apartments. What I do feel is a moral responsibility to provide as safe a living environment as possible for our residents.

I feel even more strongly about background checks after the

9/11 tragedy. When the identities of the terrorists behind the attacks as well as those who took part in the killings were revealed, several news stations reported where they lived and interviewed neighbors. In almost every instance, they lived in rental housing and many of them had fraudulent Social Security numbers, and some even had criminal backgrounds. Missed opportunities leading to a global tragedy. I background-check everyone and tell them right up front. If they don't like it, they go somewhere else and that's exactly the point.

INCREASING THE CASH FLOW

It is the property manager's responsibility to increase the cash flow of the property. Good property managers understand the real-world parameters within which they must work to achieve this goal, but if you are managing the property yourself, you'll want to be aware of what the market is doing in your immediate area. Take the time to review your local newspapers, drive by the competition, and call the surrounding properties in the area so you'll know your market before you increase your rents. Simply call and ask the rental rate, the square footage, the deposits required, and what is included in the rent.

LEGAL AND CONTRACTS

Get into the rental property business and you'll quickly learn that most states have a lot of laws governing the operations of apartments—big or small. A professional management company knows these laws and has in place the appropriate forms for residents and property owners to complete upon leasing. In addition, they know how to file the appropriate reports and documents with the government. If you do not use an outside firm, you'll need to create your own leases, eviction notices, pet addendums, and so on in accordance of the law.

Management companies also ensure that all residents are treated the same, in other words, that all have read and signed the required paperwork and are apprised of their rights as tenants and of your rights as the landlord. When you are your own property manager, especially of small properties, it's easy to be lax with your paperwork. This can and will get you into trouble eventually. If you don't believe me, rent the movie *Pacific Heights*. Not everyone is as nice as they appear on the outside.

MAINTENANCE

It's the property manager's job to maintain the landscaping, paint the apartments and the buildings, make sure all the appliances within the rental units are in good working order, and do everything including change the light bulbs in the common areas. This is all the routine stuff that makes an apartment building look like a great place to live, if it is done right, or a dump if it is neglected. It's all in the details when it comes to maintenance.

You or your property manager will receive, manage, and complete all work orders for existing residents, you'll clean the carpets, manage the trash pickup as well as coordinate or meet with all contractors for repairs. Additionally, if you are your own property manager, you'll need to source and negotiate your own providers for these services, including plumbers, electricians, carpet cleaning companies, landscapers, painters, carpenters, and so on. Property management companies typically have agreements with companies they can count on at a favored rate based on volume of work.

RENT COLLECTION

Rent collection can be an easy thing or a very challenging thing depending on the precedent you set with your residents. In the buildings my company manages, we go by the letter of the law and make no exceptions for residents who don't pay their rent on time. In this business, you have to be tough. You'll hear every story and although I feel for some of the people telling them, I also feel for the people who pay their rent on time. A property management company will operate just as I do with no gray area when it comes to collecting rent. It is easy when you are managing this aspect on your own to cut people slack and be lenient. Don't do it. Our policy is to never allow partial payments, we do not waive any late fees, and we do not accept checks from anyone who pays late more than one time. After that, we accept only money orders. Never, ever waive late fees or nonsufficient funds fees. In some cases those are the only motivators you have for residents to pay on time. Remove this and you are asking for trouble.

Realize that with every exception you make you are setting precedents. If for any reason you ever need to evict a resident for nonpayment of rent, your previous gestures of kindness may harm your case. Establish your collection policy in accordance with your state's laws and stick with them no matter what.

PAYING THE BILLS

When you own rental property, you may think you are in the accounting business. There are lots of accounting duties associated with property management. Property managers are responsible not only for collecting and depositing rent into the bank account, they also are responsible for paying all the bills on time. Every expense line item in the operating budget will have bills attached to it. Property managers you hire will take care of all monthly bills as well as all other bills that occur less frequently. At the end of each month your property manager or you should complete an analysis of the income and expenses and compare it to the budget. Do it monthly and you'll stay on top of your business.

MANAGING THE BUDGET

Along with collecting the rent and paying the bills, it is the property manager's job to manage the property's operating budget. That means that all expenses as well as rental income need to be posted and compared to the operating budget. If they come in lower, great. If they come in higher, then you'll want to know why.

There are many property management software packages that help you manage the operating budget and most of them work this way: When you enter the bills into the system for payment you code them to the correct account in your chart of accounts. Each account has a monthly allocation and when the bill is entered the software simply deducts the invoice amount from the budget, leaving you with the balance. In a way it's as if each account in the overall budget has its own checkbook register. This way, you can manage each individual account instead of just the bottom line.

Life is not perfect and there will be times that you must overspend in an account or you learn the hard way that you did not allocate enough in your budget to operate efficiently. In either case, many software programs will help you analyze how far over or under budget you are for each account. This is called a variance analysis and I do them monthly. Variance analysis reports help you see just how to adjust your spending so your bottom line stays on budget. It also is a good learning tool for future budgets you will do. Your budgets will get increasingly accurate the more you do.

EVICTIONS

Evictions are a necessary part of this business, but the good news is they don't have to be traumatic to you, the property owner. Evictions can happen for a number of reasons, including nonpayment of rent. But my company has evicted people for all sorts of reasons and it is well within our rights to do so. The only time I feel good about evicting someone is when the eviction involves drug dealers. As difficult as it is under normal circumstances, however, I never avoid the inevitable when it comes to evicting people.

Once again, a property management company that professionally manages your building will handle evictions to the letter of the law. Before you do one on your own, be sure you know your rights and the resident's rights. If you are managing your property yourself, you may want to consult with your attorney before embarking on this process.

CUSTOMER SERVICE

A big part of managing a property is being available for your residents. Residents need to know that they can call any time of the day with a problem or an emergency and that their request will be attended to in a reasonable time. This is not too much to ask; after all, if they wanted to handle their own maintenance problems they'd own their own home. This round-the-clock customer service is built into a professional property management agreement. It's something you have to provide if you manage the property on your own.

At our properties we have a twenty-four-hour policy on all non-emergency maintenance items and an immediate response on emergencies. What constitutes an emergency? For us it is fire, flood, or blood. There are certainly exceptions to this but we do not dispatch maintenance after hours for residents locked out of their apartments because they lost their key (and they do call). We have an on-call system 24/7 set up for all of our communities that is very responsive. On emergency items like a murder, we are quick to respond so that we can cooperate with the authorities and the families of the victim.

Those are just some of the job responsibilities that come with the title property manager. It is a big job that is round-the-clock, 365 days a year. If after reading this, you're thinking, Property investing isn't for me, I don't want to work that hard, take heart. Maybe property investing *is* for you. Property management *isn't*. I realize the first inclination is to want to save money so you can maximize your cash flow, but if you don't want to manage properties, that's not the place to cut corners. If a property is not managed well, it will not only make it difficult for you to find residents, it will make it difficult for you to raise your rents to market value. That will make it impossible for your asset to appreciate—after all its value is based on how it operates. Finally, hiring a professional property management company frees up your time to look for and evaluate your next property investment. As we discussed early in this book, the way to wealth is property ownership, not property management.

Poor property management is one very large contributor to a property's under-performance and reduced valuation.

Hiring a Property Management Company

If after reading this chapter so far, you are leaning toward hiring a property management company to professionally manage your property, then you'll need to know what to look for so you hire the best. Not all property management companies are created equal.

I've compiled a list of questions I ask when I'm hiring a property management company. Believe it or not, we don't self-manage all our properties. Often if we don't have a presence in a market it doesn't make sense for our management company to do the work required for just one property. So we hire it out. But as you can well imagine, we're savvy shoppers. You will be too with the list below:

• Property management fees: Fees run approximately 8–12 percent of gross rent for single-family properties and 4–8 percent depending on size for multiple-unit properties. Be skeptical of anything higher or lower.

• Time in business: I look for property management companies in business for at least three years.

• Accounting software and capabilities: I prefer to work with a company that has several people in their accounting department. A single person is a bad sign. I want to know what their accounting reports look like, when during the month they produce them, how they deliver them, and what their banking relationships are. I, of course, check the banking references.

• References: In addition to checking the banking references, I get a list of all the properties the company is managing. I personally call and visit at least five of the properties. I don't bother with general references, as no one ever gives out the names and numbers of people who will not give glowing reports.

• Policies and procedures: I ask to see their policies and procedures manual so I can understand how their organization works. This document also reveals subtleties about the company culture, management style, and employee professionalism.

• Professional affiliations and associations: The property management company should have memberships in local and national trade organizations including the National Apartment Association and the local affiliate, the Institute of Real Estate Management, the National Association of Realtors. They should also carry one or more of the following professional designations, including Certified Property Manager (CPM), Accredited Management Organization (AMO), Certified Apartment Manager (CAM), and Certified Apartment Property Supervisor (CAPS).

• Training programs: Property management requires a broad range of skills from sales to customer service to finance to legal. I look for a company that invests in its employees and provides training in those areas.

• Real estate licenses: Before I hire a property management company, I ask for copies of their state real estate licenses. If the property manager is licensed, you are protected by the government in the event of wrongdoing, such as commingling of rent moneys, and you have recourse against their license through a sanctioned government body.

• Legal and background checks: I ask for the name of the firms that the company uses for evictions and for criminal and credit background checks. I won't go with a company that does not perform background checks.

• Vendor negotiations: Property management companies need to tell me how they have negotiated with vendors to save me money on maintenance, supplies, services, advertising, everything. When you work with a large management company there should be economies of scale that mean savings to you.

• Employees: I want to know who the actual individual is that will be running my building. I expect the company to run background checks and drug tests on all employees. You need to be careful when you invite a property manager to oversee your property.

When to Fire Your Property Manager

Realize you get what you pay for in property management. And how you treat your property management company will directly affect how they treat you. This must be a relationship of mutual respect and clear accountability. There should also be mutual trust. This is a partnership, so go into it as one. If you assume an "us against them" mentality, you will lose in the long run.

A very wise man once told me that property management is a thankless job. Curious, I asked him what he meant because he clearly had many more years of experience as a professional property manager and investor. He told me the following, which I have never forgotten.

There are three basic ways a property manager can be fired.

The first way is when the property itself does not perform well, especially if the property performs worse than the investor anticipated. A change may be necessary to improve the property operations.

The second way to get fired is if the property does not improve its operations year to year or the operations remain the same. No improvement? Well, that is not why we bought the property, is it? Fire 'em!

The third way to get fired is if the property really outperforms the investor's expectations. The reason for the firing is that management looks easy and a property manager is not needed when a property is doing so well. The investor can do the job and save the fee.

What this amusing story communicates is all too true: that property managers are at the mercy of the property owners. And as a property owner you may feel pretty powerful. But don't abuse this power. Choose wisely in the first place, treat each other with respect, and stick with your property management partner. They in turn will reward you with a high level of service and the returns you are looking for. Turning your property into a revolving door of property managers is not only inefficient, it will undermine your success. Look for the long-term relationship that builds momentum and profits.

But as a property owner, you have to recognize when a property management company should be fired. These are the things I won't tolerate when it comes to property management:

- A company that doesn't assume a partner mentality and doesn't communicate to the property owner things like market conditions that affect supply and demand.

- A company that neglects the physical condition of the property. If the property manager sees a piece of litter on the ground, he or she should not step over it.

- A company that has high employee turnover in any area; this makes building a relationship difficult.

- A company that has inconsistent or incomplete reporting.

Those are valid reasons to fire your property management company. I like to set the expectation level from the very beginning, right in the management agreement. Then I discuss it with the company. Many of these expectations are regulated state by state so be aware of your state laws and do not accept any service below government standards. On the flip side, you do need to have realistic expectations. If you paid too much for the property and expect the property manager to perform miracles and bail you out, you will be disappointed.

While I may be a bit biased about property managers and the high level of service that a very good property manager can deliver, I can relate to those owners and investors who believe that property management is easy and anyone can do it. I can relate to them because these are the owners who are the focus of my property acquisitions. Invariably, properties managed by owners are full of income-generating potential because the owners just are not experienced or interested enough to manage the property right. They are prime acquisition targets.

The Domino Effect

Property management can be characterized as a whole bunch of small decisions. Make the right choices all along the way, and the road can be smooth. But make the wrong choices—take shortcuts, burn bridges, anger residents, or rip off service providers—and your challenges will be greater. You can choose to take the right path, or take the wrong path, the choice is yours. But if you chose the latter, your one bad choice can have far-reaching effects. It's like a domino effect and here are some examples of what I mean:

RENTING TO THE WRONG PERSON

We recently had a new resident who happened to be a convicted sex offender move into one of the properties we manage. This person lied on their application by checking "no" to the question that asks if they had ever been convicted of a felony.

Apparently this person moved from Texas to Arizona and broke the law by not registering with the state until *after* moving into our property. We weren't alerted to this by our criminal and credit background screening company who processed the application.

You can imagine my shock when I received the letter issued by the local police department to the neighborhood that a sex offender was living at the property. And you can imagine the anger of the residents in the community when the local authorities notified them and then the local media picked up the story.

The hundreds of residents and their families living at the property were up in arms. Obviously, we had to act fast. We fielded dozens of phone calls from our current residents worried about their children's and their own safety and the property owners had a few things to say as well. To solve the problem, I immediately contacted the resident and we discussed the situation. I agreed to take care of the moving expenses for the person, who wanted to relocate. The manager personally oversaw the move and the situation was resolved.

This kind of swift action turned a bad situation into one that actually made us stronger. We demonstrated that when concerns are raised, no matter how infrequently, we take them seriously and try to be responsive. We didn't make a big splash about the situation, we simply told people who asked that the person had moved out. Had we not taken this course of action, we would have experienced a mass exodus of good residents, guaranteed.

NOT TAKING CARE OF YOUR CURRENT RESIDENTS

There is no mystery to the trend that when you take care of your residents they are more likely to renew their leases. This is human nature. We've all had bad experiences at a hotel or department store and swore that we would never go back. It is no different in property management.

Taking care of your residents means responding to their calls quickly. It means fixing what needs to be fixed. It means a courteous, professional staff that is always happy to help. It means doing everything you would expect yourself if you were a resident. The domino effect here is that unhappy residents create vacancies and vacancies create cash flow problems. Residents talk to one another and misery loves company. Taking care of residents keeps your pool areas wonderful retreats instead of soapboxes for disgruntled residents. Parking lots stay parking lots, not common areas for gripe sessions. Be proactive and create a system that is responsive to your residents and you will keep them.

NOT BUDGETING FOR THE UNEXPECTED

Have you ever heard the phrase "*stuff* happens"? Well, I am proof that when it does, cleaning up after the mess takes longer and costs more than you always think it will. Be prepared for problems that will develop as you own a property. I'm talking about things like blown hot water tanks, floods that require new flooring and drywall, small fires that damage cabinets and appliances, compressors that fail on the hottest day of the year, broken windows, carport damage from moving companies, and wind storm damage all with repair costs that are less than your insurance deductible. Got the point?

Maintain a reserve fund that is adequate for your property for when the unexpected happens. Hopefully you never have to use it. It's hard to set guidelines for how much to put aside because every property is in a different condition when you buy it. What I do is look at this condition and flag things like older roofs or appliances that are likely to fail. Then I put aside additional funds for things that break unexpectedly.

Property management is a 365-day-a-year, twenty-four-hour-a-day job. You owe it to your residents to be available and responsive. You also owe it to yourself if you are serious about your investment appreciating and generating cash flow. This is the customer service aspect of the business and it is absolutely fundamental to your success.

People are social beings. They talk. Word gets around about the great places to live and the not so great places to live. Make sure the word on the street about your property is in the great places category. Accomplish that through your actions. Your life may be busy, but it will be a lot easier.

CHAPTER 11 ACTION STEPS

- Set up your systems for maintenance, accounting, and rent collection.

- Investigate hiring a professional property management company and interview several.

- Run criminal and credit background checks on every new applicant.

- Become involved in local supporting professional affiliations.

- Enforce the policies and procedures in the lease, no exceptions!

- Respond quickly to your residents with a smile.

Chapter 12

To Sell or Not to Sell

In an earlier chapter, we talked about the pros and cons of flipping your way to wealth. Flipping as you recall, is the act of buying property and selling it rapidly at a profit. That profit is either used to purchase another property or pocketed. Many people think this is the way to build wealth, but to me it is not. I am a firm believer in buying and holding property. That's what I do and that's how you create wealth and cash flow.

But sometimes, you will want to or need to sell your property. That doesn't mean you simply call your real estate agent and put a "For Sale" sign out on the street. It requires some strategy. Just as you want to manage your property to maximize cash flow, you'll want to sell your property to maximize your return on investment. That means you'll want to sell your property at the highest price possible.

And if you've learned anything from this book, hopefully you've learned that the price of a property is based on its operations.

By now you will have already done your management plan which guides you as you manage your property to maximize its cash flow. That's great. That's what a management plan should do. Of course you're using it daily. Referring to it often. And updating it annually, aren't you? Well, maybe not annually. In truth if you're like most people, once your building is occupied and running well, you may not remember where the building is, let alone where the management plan is. It's scary but it happens. I'm not endorsing that type of absentee ownership, of course!

So, if you are an absentee owner, find the management plan, dust it off, and take a look at it. You'll need this to prepare your property for sale. This entire book has trained you to view and evaluate properties as a buyer. But to sell your property, you have to view it as a seller. Remember the discussion about retail and wholesale? Buyers want to buy property at wholesale, and sellers want to sell it at retail. This chapter will show you how to have as much of your operations at the *retail* level to bring you the highest sale price possible. How do you do that? There are two basic methods.

Maximize Your Future Potential Income

When you are buying and holding property it makes sense to want to maximize your cash flow. After all, you want to reap an annual return for years to come, and the higher the better. To do that you'll want your property at 100 percent occupancy, even if it means some of your rents are slightly below market.

However, when you are planning to sell your property, you want your rental rates to be at the market rate in the area. This is because the value of the property will be based upon not necessarily the current income, but the future potential income of the property. Sometimes there is a very big difference between the two. When you are selling your property, you want to demonstrate the highest future potential income for the property, not the highest actual income, because remember, as explained in Chapter 7, the actual income is the wholesale price, potential income is the retail price. As the seller, you want to sell at as close to retail as possible, even at the expense of occupancy!

Let me explain: No buyer will buy your property with the assumption that it will be 100 percent occupied forever. If they do, please have them e-mail me immediately, I have swampland I'd like to show them. Rather, buyers must understand there will always be a vacancy component in the analysis, which could be as low as 2 percent and I have seen it as high as 20 percent. Regardless of the number, the point I'm trying to make is that when you are selling your property it is not always to your benefit to be at 100 percent occupancy. When I'm buying a property, 100 percent occupancy to me means that the rents are too low or the seller is trying to pull one over on me.

> *To maximize your sale price, you are*
> *better off having your market rents*
> *high and creating some vacancy.*

Let me give you an example. If your twenty-unit property was 100 percent occupied and the rents were an average of $35 lower per unit when compared to the market rents in the area, you would be losing $700 in rent per month (assuming again you were at 100 percent occupancy). You've left $8,400 in annual cash flow for the next buyer ($700 per month multiplied by 12 months). This short-fall goes straight to the bottom line, and remember the bottom line determines the ultimate value of the property.

Going back to our formula for calculating the offer price of a property, you know that the offer price equals the net operating income divided by the capitalization rate. Using a conservative capitalization rate of 10 percent, divided into the $8,400 in cash flow left on the table, you would experience an $84,000 reduction in your purchase price. Just from having your rents $35 per unit too low!

As I mentioned before, buyers will assume there will be some vacancy, so they will assign a 5–7 percent vacancy rate on your property even if it is currently 100 percent occupied or not.

You can see how impossible it becomes to get top dollar for your property if your rents are below-market. Sometimes it is difficult to have all the rents in line with the market, but you should at least have some of them at that level. If you do not have one unit with rents at market and your buyer read this book, you'll find yourself on the other side of the valuation discussion we outlined in Chapter 7. That's not a good place to be. At that point, your only alternatives will be to sell your property low, or hold on to it and prepare it for sale by increasing your rents and therefore the future operation's performance potential.

Your team members can help you update your market rent information. Management company and broker contacts will be particularly helpful. I must emphasize, however, that to be successful in this business, you need to know this information on an ongoing basis. You can see from the example above how quickly a small $35 rent difference can result in loss of cash flow and loss of value. This is a business you'll want to stay on top of.

Now that you know the importance of maximizing the future potential income of the property, you're probably wondering how you accomplish it. There are two ways:

- You re-rent vacancies at the market rent (retail).

- You renew your current resident leases at the market rent (retail).

Don't be alarmed if these actions create vacancies and turnover. In some cases they will. But remember, you are not managing to maximize cash flow here. You are managing the property for sale and that means you want to demonstrate the property's highest potential income. You can only do that by demonstrating your rental units can command rents at the market level. The more units you can move to market level rents, the smaller the gap between wholesale and retail. The smaller the gap, the easier it will be for you to get a retail price for your property.

Running Your Expenses Lean

The next area to manage when you want to sell your property is your expenses. There are two kinds of expenses: fixed and variable. The fixed expenses are your property taxes, utilities, insurance. The variable expenses are management costs, payroll, administrative, advertising, repairs, and maintenance items. You'll have a lot more impact on the variable expenses, so you'll want to focus on those first. The goal is to minimize them as much as possible. Not for the sake of being a cheapskate, but for the purpose of showing that you can operate the property with the lowest possible expenses.

Remember, as a buyer you will be looking at the expenses of the properties you buy and will likely be estimating them higher. Now, as the seller, you'll want to demonstrate the lowest possible operating expenses. In fact, when I'm positioning a property for sale, we'll minimize staff members, reduce or cancel advertising, and raise the deductible on the insurance all in an effort to minimize the expenses. It's nothing complicated, but it can make a big difference in the sale price of your property.

Look hard at the management plan you created during due diligence. Are you still taking advantage of every cost-saving tactic you outlined in the plan? Look at everything, including the small things; they add up. Bid out all your services again, adjust your rents to reflect location premiums, have your landscaper visit only one time per week instead of two. Be as diligent now as you were when buying your property.

Seek Out Qualified Buyers

Once you have your property positioned for sale, you'll want to seek out qualified buyers. For some reason, some sellers like to be secretive about selling their property. Maybe they expect a drop in the level of property management service if the management company knows the property will be changing hands. A good property management company will help you by creating value if they know the goals of the ownership.

Whether you manage the property yourself or use a professional company you need to communicate to everyone your goal of selling the property. What some of my property management clients don't understand is that we are working with many investors and owners of property within our own company. Property management companies are a prime source of leads, so you are wise to take advantage of the network. There have been times when we've found buyers for properties we manage. If you are working with a large management company that is reputable and successful, there will not be any hardship associated with the loss of one management account. Again, this is a relationship business and if the company was doing a good job, they know you'll seek them out on the next property you purchase.

There is a time for confidentiality of course, and that time is when you are actually approached by a prospective buyer. You'll want to have a confidentiality agreement ready for the prospect to sign before you disclose anything to him or her. This protects both of you.

What to Do with Your Money

If you do sell your property, you need a plan for what to do with your money. I have a friend who had a small property in San Diego. Although the property was not listed for sale, he was approached by a prospective buyer. They made an offer for a sum of money way higher than what he paid for the property. He took the deal and decided to sell. Unfortunately at the time, the San Diego apartment market was really hot and he could not find another deal that was worthy of reinvesting his money. Had he known that at the time, he might have thought twice about taking the offer. To avoid a large tax bill on his huge capital gain, he was forced to look in other markets in other cities and states to reinvest his money.

Now he is out of his comfort zone. He has had to quickly assemble a team, learn another market, actually multiple markets, visit numerous potential properties, all while working at another job. This deal threw his life into total upheaval. And the clock was ticking. On exchanges such as this, you have a limited amount of time to reinvest the money and declare it tax-free. He had to cut corners on things like assembling his team and even due diligence. He barreled headlong into a property he didn't know enough about, just to avoid the big tax bite. It was the wrong property, bought too high and with a lot of deferred maintenance. It was a bad deal, but one he had little choice but to take.

My point is not to slam the practices of this investor, but to warn future sellers that if you don't have a plan for your capital gain, you should not sell the property. It is easy to be lured by the cash. If you are truly a property investor, you will likely have irons in the fire and have some properties on the horizon. That's great. But if you are a passive investor with no properties in process, you may have to scramble and be left with a bad investment or a large tax liability.

I would never sell a property without having at least three or four deals in the works for which I could use the money to reinvest. That's the only way to prevent a hefty tax bill and avoid making foolish decisions that will cost you money in both the short and long run.

A Final Word

There will come a day when the properties my partner and I own will be sold. But until that day, the cash flow generated from them, and their appreciation in value, ensures that we have the ability to do the things we love today, and in the future. There is a freedom that comes with that knowledge. It was what I was searching for when I set my own personal goal of financial freedom. Little did I know that the freedom would go far beyond the dollars. Freedom to spend time with my family. Freedom to do the things that I want to do. Freedom to share my experiences with others. Property investing—particularly buying and holding property—started out as a means to an end. But it has become something much more. It is an end in itself and a thrilling journey.

Ken McElroy

Ken McElroy has been a property management advisor to the Rich Dad organization since 2001 and has spoken in various cities throughout the United States and Australia. Ken has created the audio tape series, "How to Increase the Income from your Real Estate Investments – Secrets of Professional Property Managers." Ken has nearly twenty years of multifamily investment and management experience, overseeing over 20,000 apartment units.

Ken co-manages The MC Companies, which is located in Arizona and has investments throughout the Western United States. The MC Companies is a group of companies formed to acquire, develop, construct, manage and convert multifamily property through out the Western United States, for themselves and for various investors. MC Companies current management and investment portfolio consists of over 4,000 units with a market value of over $250,000,000 (www.mccompanies.com).

Ken is currently on the Board of Directors acting as the Regional Vice President of the National Apartment Association for region seven, which encompasses eight Western States. He is the 2004 Chairman of the Board for the Arizona Multihousing Association.

Ken is also an active member of the World Entrepreneurs Organization and Young Entrepreneurs Organization, holding several board positions including President for the upcoming fiscal year of 2004-2005.

**Robert Kiyosaki's Edumercial
An Educational Commercial**

The Three Incomes

In the world of accounting, there are three different types of income: earned, passive and portfolio. When my real dad said to me, "Go to school, get good grades and find a safe secure job," he was recommending I work for earned income. When my rich dad said, "The rich don't work for money, they have their money work for them," he was talking about passive income and portfolio income. Passive income, in most cases, is derived from real estate investments. Portfolio income is income derived from paper assets, such as stocks, bonds, and mutual funds.

Rich dad used to say, "The key to becoming wealthy is the ability to convert earned income into passive income and/or portfolio income as quickly as possible." He would say, "The taxes are highest on earned income. The least taxed income is passive income. That is another reason why you want your money working hard for you. The government taxes the income you work hard for - more than the income your money works hard for."

The Key to Financial Freedom

The key to financial freedom and great wealth is a person's ability or skill to convert earned income into passive income and/or portfolio income. That is the skill that my rich dad spent a lot of time teaching Mike and me. Having that skill is the reason my wife Kim and I are financially free, never needing to work again. We continue to work because we choose to. Today we own a real estate investment company for passive income and participate in private placements and initial public offerings of stock for portfolio income.

Investing to become rich requires a different set of personal skills – skills essential for financial success as well as low-risk and high-investment returns. In other words, knowing how to create assets that buy other assets. The problem is that gaining the basic education and experience required is often time consuming, frightening, and expensive, especially when you make mistakes with your own money. That is why I created the patented educational board games trademarked as CASHFLOW®.

The New York Times

writes:

"Move over, Monopoly®...
A new board game that
aims to teach people how
to get rich is gaining fans
the world over!"

WHY PLAY GAMES?

Games are a **powerful learning tool** because they enable people to experience 'hands-on' learning. As a **true reflection of behavior**, games are a **window to our attitudes**, our **abilities to see opportunities**, and **assess risk and rewards**.

Each of the CASHFLOW® games creates a forum in which to evaluate life decisions regarding money and finances and immediately see the results of your decisions.

**Play often and learn
what it takes to
*get out of the
Rat Race-*
for good!**

RichKidSmartKid.com

Money is a life skill---but we don't teach our children about money in school. I am asking for your help in getting financial education into the hands of interested teachers and school administrators.

RichKidSmartKid.com was created as an innovative and interactive Web site designed to convey key concepts about money and finance in ways that are fun and challenging...and educational for young people in grades K through 12. It contains 4 mini-games that teach:

Assets vs. Liabilities
Good Debt vs. Bad Debt
Importance of Charity
Passive Income vs. Earned Income

AND, schools may also register at www.richkidsmartkid.com to receive a FREE download of our electronic version of CASHFLOW for Kids at School.

How You Can Make a Difference

Play CASHFLOW for KIDs and CASHFLOW 101 with family and friends and share the richkidsmartkid.com Web site with your local teachers and school administrators.

Join me now in taking financial education to our schools and e-mail me of your interest at Iwill@richdad.com. Together we can better prepare our children for the financial world they will face.

Thank you!

DISCOVER THE POWER OF THESE RICH DAD PROGRAMS:

• Rich Dad's You Can Choose to Be Rich

• Rich Dad's 6 Steps to Becoming a Successful Real Estate Investor

• Rich Dad's How to Increase the Income from Your Real Estate Investments

Step-by-step guides with audio components and comprehensive workbooks ensure that you can take the knowledge you gain and apply it to increasing the value and profitability of your investment portfolio.

"Because of Rich Dad, I've learned that wealth is all around us. It's accessible and attainable. You can read books, you can seek advice...but playing the CASHFLOW game put things into perspective for me. It awakened the concept of becoming wealthy, of how rich people think, and what they do. This makes me want to continue my financial education to make a better life for my family."

– Roshiem A., Arizona

"Our children, Madeline (4 years old) and Makenzie (3 years old), absolutely love the interactive programs from Rich Dad. Madeline is already gaining real knowledge regarding investment and money matters through "Rich Kid, Smart Kid," which I find to be amazing at her age. It also provides a forum for me, as a parent, to begin discussing and teaching some of these concepts to my small children – something I probably would not do at this stage if it were not for your program."

– Jon F., Arizona

"The concepts taught by Robert Kiyosaki and the Rich Dad Team have had a major impact on our lives and our business. As tax and business consultants, the ways we serve our clients have changed and improved considerably. Everyone in our office now thinks in terms of "doodads" and cash flow and getting out of the Rat Race on a daily basis."

"One of the greatest impacts on our clients has been the CASHFLOW 101 game. For years, we have been looking for ways to instruct clients on accounting principals and tax strategies. CASHFLOW 101 is a terrific instructional tool for these concepts, as well as general investing and financial management. We play CASHFLOW 101 with clients and friends of the firm every month. These game nights give our clients the opportunity to broaden their perspective on money and investing, while allowing us to help them understand basic accounting principals, money management, and tax strategies."

"Thank you for creating a marvelous teaching tool in CASHFLOW 101 and helping us change the way we look at finances for ourselves and for our clients."

– Tom W. and Ann M., Arizona

"I was a project manager/engineer and had worked my way up the corporate ladder for 20 years. I was finally making good money only to find that I was getting killed on taxes. On top of that, I could not picture myself working 9-to-5 for another 30 years."

"After reading Rich Dad's Guide to Investing, it dawned on me that I was directing an engineering team at work. So why not orchestrate my own real estate investment team? My team of advisors now consists of two lawyers, an accountant, two real estate brokers, an insurance agent, three mortgage brokers, a home inspector and – one of the strongest players on the team – my wife and partner, Connie. Life's too short to shortchange yourself."

– Larry N., Mass.

What Others Are Saying About Rich Dad...

"A friend of mine introduced me to the Rich Dad books a few years ago, and I introduced them to my Dad, a farmer who was just beginning to invest in real estate. My Dad and I then gave books and tapes to my sisters...and the family was hooked!"

"We recently closed on four townhouses (a "deal" my Dad found by being open to opportunities...) and know we never would have been thinking about cash flow and passive income if we hadn't read the Rich Dad books. We all financed our properties differently and our returns on investment vary – but we're all moving in the right direction."

"It is so exciting to constantly stretch and change the way we think about money."

– Sally D., California

"Thanks to Rich Dad I have the courage and confidence to tackle life's Big Deal cards – and create true financial freedom."

– Cindy O., Texas

"We were realtors focused only on earning our commissions. And when we first heard of the book Rich Dad Poor Dad – from a "recommended reading" list given to us by our business coach – we realized that we were SELLING all the best deals...instead of capturing them for ourselves!"

"Thanks to Rich Dad we began to focus on the cash flow of our properties (instead of commissions) and ways in which we could leverage those properties to acquire more. Traveling the road to financial freedom has been an enlightening ride!"

– Curtis and Diana O., California

"A year ago I was drowning in bad debt and considering bankruptcy. I was frustrated and angry. My financial state of affairs — my financial ignorance — nearly cost me my family, my business, and my self respect."

"Rich Dad Poor Dad had such a powerful impact on me that I've bought a dozen copies and gave them to my staff, my friends, and my college-age children. As a business owner, Rich Dad's Cashflow Quadrant helped me understand the BI Triangle and taught me to create and implement systems that strengthen my business."

"My Money IQ is rising everyday and I can say, honestly, that the Rich Dad messages have saved me from financial ruin."

– Dr. Randy R., Ohio

What Others Are Saying About Rich Dad...

"A huge thanks to Robert for helping me shift my context. It has made a huge change in how I view the world. I have been reading your materials, listening to audios, and playing your CASHFLOW games for over a year now. It has helped me grow my financial literacy so much that my husband and I have begun investing in real estate. We just purchased our first property!"

– Valerie P., Canada

"The Rich Dad books have been a life-changing experience for me. Robert has given me the faith and courage to follow my convictions and prepare my plan for financial freedom. The Rich Dad books have given me the courage to take the steps to financial freedom."

"I have purchased two properties apart from my residence and while it's tempting to repay my mortgages, I intend to leverage the equity from these properties to invest in others."

– Kay G., United Kingdom

"Thanks to inspiration from Robert and Sharon, our lives will be different from 99% of the population."

"You have been our guiding light in our quest for financial freedom. Playing the CASHFLOW game has taught me more about business than business school did! You are making a huge difference in this world of financial illiteracy and chaos."

– Merced, Jon, and Jeff H., Utah

What Students and Teachers Are Saying About CASHFLOW for Kids

"They can learn more in an hour of playing Cashflow for Kids than 10 hours of homework."

– Pam L. - Principal, Oklahoma

"I feel sorry for my mom, because (credit card debt) is hard to get out of and easy to get in."

– Carrie S. – 6th grader, Oklahoma

"One teacher asked the kids, 'If money was no object, what would you buy?' At the beginning of the day they wanted a car and by the end of the day they wanted a candy bar factory or other things to make money with."

– Michelle H., Scottsdale